THE
DELAWARE
CANAL

THE
DELAWARE
CANAL

FROM STONE COAL HIGHWAY
TO HISTORIC LANDMARK

MARIE MURPHY DUESS

Charleston   London

THE
History
PRESS

Published by The History Press
Charleston, SC 29403
www.historypress.net

Cover design by Marshall Hudson.

Cover image: Fred Wagner, *Canal at Lumberville*, circa 1910, oil on canvas, 20 x 24 inches. *James A. Michener Art Museum. Gift of Marguerite and Gerry Lenfest.*

First published 2008

Manufactured in the United States

ISBN 978.1.59629.487.5

Library of Congress Cataloging-in-Publication Data

Duess, Marie Murphy.
The Delaware Canal : from stone coal highway to historic landmark / Marie Murphy Duess.
p. cm.
Includes bibliographical references.
ISBN 978-1-59629-487-5
1. Delaware Canal (Pa.)--History. 2. Canals--Pennsylvania--History. 3. Coal--Transportation--Pennsylvania--History--19th century. 4. National parks and reserves--Pennsylvania. I. Title.
HE396.D33D84 2008
386'.480974821--dc22
2008021049

To the Americans—born and bred and immigrant alike—who "worked" the Delaware Canal…the laborers who built the canal with nothing more than shovels and picks…the pilots who steered the snappers and stiff boats through all that nature threw at them…the lock tenders who worked from four o'clock in the morning until ten o'clock at night…and the mule drivers (mostly children and often in bare feet) who guided the mules more than sixty miles each way eight months a year. Their stories are inspiring, moving and legendary.

And, as always, to Ed, Mai and Buddy—my history and my future—and to Tommy and Christian, my best guys.

Genius is present in every age, but the men carrying it within them remain benumbed unless extraordinary events occur to heat up and melt the mass so that it flows forth.
—Denis Diderot

Contents

Foreword, by James C. Greenwood   11

Preface   13

Acknowledgements   15

Chapter 1   Magic Canals: Past and Future   17

Chapter 2   From the Bowels of the Earth   25

Chapter 3   Josiah White's Waterways   45

Chapter 4   Locks and Their Keepers   53

Chapter 5   Beside the Busy Canal   65

Chapter 6   Snappers and Stiff Boats   75

Chapter 7   The Mules   85

Chapter 8   The Canallers   97

Chapter 9   Human Cargo   117

Chapter 10   The Canal's Worst Enemy   127

Chapter 11   Beautiful Impressions   131

Chapter 12   National Historic Landmark   137

Notes   151

Bibliography and Resources   155

Index   157

Foreword

For a century the Delaware Canal served as a man-made working waterway, floating three thousand flat-bottomed, mule-drawn boats brimming with coal, lumber and manufactured goods along the sixty-mile route from Easton to the river port in Bristol in a rapidly industrializing eastern Pennsylvania.

From 1832 to 1931 men, women and children—Irish and German immigrants, former slaves and others—eked out livings on the hustle-bustle, hardscrabble, but colorful world of the canalboats until that world gave way with the advent of the freight train.

Its working days over, the Delaware Canal has served us still in its retirement for more than three-quarters of another century. Threatened with deteriorating locks and gates, leaks and abandonment; insulted by highway and railroad crossings; paved over with a shopping center's parking lot; and repeatedly battered by a recent series of raging floods, the canal has yet endured, rescued repeatedly by the affection and commitment of its more recent travelers.

Hikers and bikers, handholding lovers, bird watchers and dog walkers, painters and picnickers, locals and visitors, kids toting fishing poles, parents with strollers—we come with cross-country skis, canoes and cameras to rest and to play. And sometimes, when reminded, as we are in Marie Duess's excellent work, we think of our forebears who plied these waters from before dawn until well past dark.

I have been privileged to live and to raise my family beside the canal for thirty years. As an elected official I have worked with the Friends of the Delaware Canal and other dedicated citizens who have refused to surrender our special treasure to apathy, abuse or catastrophe. While some have called to pave it, we have fought to save it. And save it we will.

The Delaware Canal is as central to Bucks County's story as William Penn's home or Washington's Crossing. Uniquely, it is a park, a National

Historic Landmark and a charming, natural pathway winding its way through our beloved picturesque and historic villages. We are fortunate to call this treasure our own and to share it with those who come from afar.

And so we have a duty to preserve it for our children so that they may pass it on to theirs.

James C. Greenwood
President and CEO of Biotechnology Industry Organization
United States House of Representatives (1993–2005)

Preface

While doing the research for this book, I fell in love with Bucks County all over again—just as I did twenty-one years ago when my husband and I moved our family to this lovely place, and again in 2007 when I learned so much more about the county in which I live while writing *Colonial Inns and Taverns of Bucks County: How Pubs, Taprooms and Hostelries Made Revolutionary History*. Bucks County has a fascinating history and is a captivating place to live.

I have also become enamored with mules since writing this book. I had no idea what interesting animals they are. I always thought they were beautiful, but I didn't know they were intelligent, too—gentle when treated kindly and spiteful when wronged—and not stubborn at all, but just smart enough to know when their loads are too heavy and it is time to rest. We humans could take a lesson from them where that is concerned.

There is so much in this book that I relate to. Although this book is about the Lehigh mines and the Delaware Division Canal, my mother's family is from the anthracite coal region of Carbondale, Pennsylvania—the site of the first underground mine in the United States, developed before the Lehigh mines and home to the founders of the Delaware and Hudson Canal Company. Throughout my life I heard many stories about the mines and miners, and I was always fascinated by stories I was told about the mine fire that burned for years beneath the streets of Carbondale. I didn't know about the breaker boys, however, and wish I didn't have to. Their story breaks my heart.

My Irish-American Catholic father told me about the discrimination his mother and father experienced when they first arrived in New York from the "old country" in the early twentieth century. They were branded as drunks and fighters before they had a chance to prove themselves different; yet both were gentle, loving and kind.

I cried when I wrote about the fleeing slaves who hid in subterranean rooms, living in constant fear of being caught, wondering what danger was just around the next corner. Being claustrophobic myself, I could almost feel the panic they must have experienced when they had to crawl through underground tunnels and hide in windowless chambers. Their courage is inspirational, and their stories remind me that freedom is precious and should never be taken for granted.

When writing this book, I could almost hear the boatmen calling out to the lock tenders as they worked the canal and the bells on the mules' harnesses as they walked the towpath beside their drivers. I have to smile when I think of the barefoot children walking along the canal on beautiful summer days, yet I wince when I remember that they also walked in the rain, cold and snow.

I wish I could go back in time, if just for an hour, to walk the canal as it was then, wave to the boat captains, touch the cheek of a little mule driver, give some tobacco to a mule and peek over the shoulder of Redfield or Coppedge as they capture the canal in a masterpiece.

The canal age was an important era in our country's development. The stories in this book speak to the work ethic of a different day and the cultural differences that have, for the most part, now become our American identity.

As I have with the county in which it is located, I also have fallen in love with the Delaware Division Canal. I hope that after reading this book, you will fall in love with it, too, and will be drawn to Bucks County's beautiful historic treasure as I am.

Acknowledgements

My most sincere appreciation is extended to:

My wonderful editor, Saunders Robinson, for her confidence in me, and to all the people at The History Press who seem to make things happen almost effortlessly.

Jim Greenwood, for taking the time out of his busy schedule to write the beautiful foreword for this book and for his, and his wife Tina's, gracious hospitality in allowing me to do some research in their lovely historic home and stables along the canal.

Charles Lauble Jr., of the Historic Langhorne Association, for all of his assistance and support—he is extraordinary.

Millard C. Mitchell, who is painstakingly keeping alive the stories of the underground railroad in Lower Bucks County—he is truly a great gentleman and historian.

The New Hope Historical Society, especially Barry Ziff, for his help, his stories and his expertise.

The Grundy Library, for all of their assistance in my research.

The National Canal Museum in Easton, for their assistance in obtaining photographs for this book, especially Ann Bartholomew and Susan E. Francisco—without their help, this book would not be as visually interesting.

Friends of the Delaware Canal, especially Susan Taylor, who shared the Friends' dreams for the canal.

Rosemary Tottoroto, a wonderful artist, for sharing her photographs and experience in designing one of Bucks County's "icon" mules.

Paul and Harriet Gratz of Gratz Gallery in New Hope and Sara Buehler of the Michener Museum—they all went above and beyond in helping me obtain images of the paintings of our American impressionists who so loved the Delaware Canal.

Robin G. Lightly, Mineral Resources program manager of the Bureau of Mining and Reclamation, for sharing her moving—and sobering—images of the children and men who worked the mines in Pennsylvania.

Frank Lyons of the Continental Tavern, for sharing information about the historic tavern and allowing me to *experience* the secret room that protected the courageous and hopeful Americans who sought freedom before the Civil War.

Greg Chalson…just because.

Finally, to the historians who keep the stories of the canal era alive through their writing and lectures, especially Lance Metz, Albright G. Zimmerman, C.P. Yoder, James Lee, William H. Shank, Will Rivinus, Terry McNealy, Robert J. McClellan and the New Hope Canal Boat Company, especially "Captain" Dave and his mule driver, Charles.

Chapter 1

Magic Canals

Past and Future

Canals hold a special place in the hearts of the people who live near or work on them. Their tranquil beauty and history inspire protectiveness. Ancient canals are considered sacred, and like the people and organizations in modern times that fight to preserve the canals in their communities, there is evidence that people in medieval times fought just as fiercely to safeguard their own man-made waterways.

Canals are charismatic. People flock to France, England, Germany and other parts of Europe and Asia to vacation on boats that float gracefully down some of the most beautiful and ancient canals in the world, moving through old stone locks, passing orchards, farms and fragrant vineyards.

People who live by canals find themselves walking at a different pace during an early morning or evening stroll. They revel in the vibrancy of colors reflected off the water; they experience a quiet peace from the harmony that exists between the lush vegetation and the wildlife that is sustained by it. There is always something at which to marvel. There is, in fact, something *magical* about canals.

Canals of China

Although irrigation canals have been in existence since the sixth millennium BCE in Mesopotamia and Egypt, and as early as 4000 BCE in other areas of the Middle East, the first transportation canal was built in China in the third century BCE. Called *Lingqu*—"Magic Canal"—it is an impressive achievement in engineering and longevity. When Emperor Qin Shih Huangdi needed a way to transport supplies inland to his armies, he employed the genius of engineer Shi Lu, who built his Magic Canal to link the Rivers Xiang and Li, which ran in opposite directions. The success and durability of the Lingqu laid the groundwork for additional canals in

The Grand Canal of China is the longest ancient canal in the world. *Courtesy of Istockphotos. com.*

ancient China. Joseph Needham, the author of *Science and Civilisation* [sic] *in China*, noted, "Few if any other civilisations [*sic*] could demonstrate a work of hydraulic art in continuous use for well over two thousand years."[1] Indeed, the Magic Canal is still used today and is considered a sacred waterway, with a dragon as its governing spirit.[2]

In AD 604, when Yang Guang ascended the throne of China, he ordered the completion of what was to be called the Grand Canal. Measuring 1,115 miles long and 100 miles wide, the Grand Canal was completed in 609, combined many older canals and is, to this day, the longest canal in the world. Its construction supposedly took the work of more than two million men.[3]

Roman Aqueducts

Throughout their vast empire, the ancient Romans were industrious aqueduct and canal builders, and these structures are excellent examples of the engineering of the ancient world. They built aqueducts to supply fresh water to the largest cities in their empire, normally routing them below ground to keep the water from being tainted by the lack of sanitary conditions above.

When wars died down during the first two centuries AD, Roman leaders kept their troops occupied with military construction and put them to work improving the previously neglected infrastructures. Roman military engineers were skilled surveyors and designed vast projects in the Roman provinces. They built networks of roads, bridges and canals that opened commerce and cultural influences with many regions that had previously been unreachable. Even Syrians refer to their ancient canals as *qanats Romani* or "Roman canals," although archaeological evidence and written accounts suggest they were first established by the Persians in Syria.[4]

The Foss Dyke in England is the oldest canal built by the Romans in that country. It was constructed in AD 120 and, like the Chinese canals, is still in use today, largely for pleasure trips. In contrast to the 1,115-mile-long Grand Canal of China, the Foss Dyke is only 11 miles long, but its history is just as rich. The Danes invaded England by way of the canal, and the Normans used it to carry stone to build the medieval Lincoln Cathedral in 1072. This canal was so important to England's residents that Katherine Swynford, the mistress and eventual third wife of John of Gaunt, the first Duke of Lancaster, organized a protest to repair the Foss Dyke in 1375 after its severe deterioration.[5]

Canals have been built and used throughout Europe. Some of the most beautiful and photographed canals are in Venice and Holland, where they are even more important than roadways for transportation.

A Place in the Future

We look at canals as designs of engineering genius that were important for *ancient* trading routes started by the Romans, Persians and Greeks and that played a significant role in the eighteenth and nineteenth centuries to set in motion the Industrial Revolution of England and America. But the truth is, canals may reemerge as a viable source of transportation in the twenty-first century.

The Seine-Nord Europe Canal, which will link the Seine River in France to northern Europe, is scheduled to begin construction in 2008. It is estimated that it will transport thirty-two million tons of goods annually, employing modern and efficient shipping vessels. Because this inland waterway will consume very little energy in comparison to the fuel needed to transport goods by truck, ship and rail, and due to the fact that it will be low in atmospheric and noise pollution, it is expected to have little negative impact on the environment. It is being managed by Voies Navigables de France (VNF), and will take approximately five years to complete.[6] Additionally, some canals are being used as wayleaves for fiber-optic telecommunications networks.[7]

It is not impossible, therefore, to imagine that canals will come back as a modern, safe and environmentally sound means of transporting goods and people just as they were in the past.

Waterways of America

William Penn wanted a canal system one hundred years before the American Revolution. George Washington thought it was a good idea when he was just a young surveyor. So did Benjamin Franklin. Yet it wasn't until 1800 that canals started to become a means of commercial transportation in the United States.

America was a very young country, with the bulk of our settled land stretching along the Atlantic coast. We needed to push westward to access the rich natural resources that lay beyond the early boundaries of our colonies, but most of the roadways were barely passable—not much more than Native American paths too narrow for wagons.

The industrial use of canals was in full force in Europe late in the eighteenth century. Around 1796, Pennsylvanian Robert Fulton, who invented the first successful steamboat, spent time in England to study its canal systems. He maintained constant communication with George Washington, who was president at that time, and Governor John Mifflin of Pennsylvania. Excited about the achievements in canal building in England, Fulton promoted the establishment of canals in the new country.

His enthusiasm impressed President Washington, who founded the Patowmack Company to make improvements in the navigability of the Potomac River. Once established, the company built canals that skirted the major falls and allowed boats and rafts to float downstream toward Georgetown. Moving *upriver*, against the current, was more difficult, however.

The first notable American canal project began in 1793 with the chartering of the Middlesex Canal in Massachusetts by Governor John Hancock. Upon completion in 1803, this twenty-seven-mile canal connected the Merrimack River with the port of Boston.

New York, Maryland, Pennsylvania, Virginia and the Carolinas all began to investigate the viability of man-made waterways. In 1810, New York laid plans to build a canal from Albany to Lake Ontario, but these plans were waylaid by the onset of the War of 1812. When construction began again in 1817, it was decided to change the direction of the canal route and travel to Lake Erie, near Buffalo, bypassing Lake Ontario, where there were still some hostilities. Completed in 1825 and called the Erie Canal, this waterway opened the route from the Hudson River in New York City to the Great Lakes. As a result, New York City suddenly became one of the world's most important seaports, and the "canal age" in this country began in full force with the support of millions of dollars of government money, bonds purchased by foreign banking houses and a few private American investors.

The introduction of canals resulted in the country's first tunnels, launched the need for additional engineering and scientific inventions and set the precedent for eminent domain. But the engineering and building of these first man-made waterways in America was not easy. At the time that the Erie Canal was built, West Point was the only college that offered engineering. Most of America's canals were built by trial and error and were overseen by inventors, lawyers and bankers with no engineering education. Not until the Erie Canal was completed did Harvard, Yale, Dartmouth and other Ivy League schools in the nation introduce engineering courses.

Although very few remnants of the canal age remain intact in this country, at its height there were five thousand miles of canals stretching across the United States that opened trade in major marketplaces for once-isolated farmers and manufacturers. The country's mule-drawn canalboats transported adventurers and immigrants and the goods they needed to expand the nation westward, while cargoes of coal, grain and lumber were brought to the East to feed the Industrial Revolution. The canal age's contribution to the history of this nation is undeniable, even if mostly forgotten.

The Pennsylvania Canals

When King Charles II gave a charter to establish a colony in America to William Penn, it was in payment for a debt owed to Penn's father. The king called the land the "Woods of Penn"—or "Pennsylvania"—and appointed William the proprietor of the land, accountable to the king directly.

A Quaker who had suffered greatly in England because of his conversion to the Society of Friends, Penn longed for a place where people could worship according to their own consciences. He was a man with great vision, deep spirituality, intelligence and idealism. And although he was a modest man who lived according to the dictates of the Society of Friends, he was one of the colonies' greatest diplomats.

Even before leaving for America, Penn had developed the First Frame of Government, which provided religious tolerance as well as secured private property, unlimited free enterprise, a free press and trial by jury. Upon arriving in America in 1682 aboard the *Welcome*, he immediately began plans for the first Pennsylvania city of Philadelphia. When it was completed, it became one of the country's first and busiest seaports.

During that time, Penn proposed another settlement that would be located on the Susquehanna River, where he believed it would be possible to establish a branch of the river that would open up trade and transportation by water to the west and northwest. Unfortunately, the canal he proposed in 1690 was not built.

Shortly after he arrived in the colonies, Penn needed to return to England, and although he directed the progress of Pennsylvania from his estates in Ireland and England, he could not return to Pennsylvania until 1699. Two years later he was again forced to return to England, where Parliament was threatening to terminate his proprietorship. Although he always intended to return to what he considered his home, he never did. Though many of his plans—including the Holy Experiment, as he called it—continued in his absence, William Penn was never to enjoy its success personally.

Between 1762 and 1770, renowned American astronomer, inventor, mathematician and surveyor David Rittenhouse and Dr. William Smith, the provost of the University of Pennsylvania, surveyed the route that connected

William Penn (1644–1718), founder and proprietor of the colony King George II called Pennsylvania, was a Quaker and renowned diplomat and statesman. *Courtesy of Pennsbury Manor.*

the Susquehanna and Delaware Valleys that Penn had proposed. That route later became the Union Canal, and in fact was the first canal to be surveyed in the United States, even though it wasn't the first to be built. Construction began in 1792 during George Washington's administration (he turned the first shovel of earth), and approximately fifteen miles were completed. Work stopped on the canal when the company building it suffered financial difficulties, and it did not begin again for twenty-seven years.[8]

The Pennsylvania legislature authorized a lottery to raise funds for the completion of the canal in 1795, and although it was the most significant canal lottery in United States history, more prize money was given out than funds raised to give to the canal company for production and construction purposes.

The enthusiasm to build canals in Pennsylvania seemed to have declined after that. Then, when a very important discovery was made in the mountains of Pennsylvania, indifference to canals turned into necessity—and in the case of the Pennsylvania canals, necessity truly was the mother of invention.

Chapter 2

From the Bowels of the Earth

Raking Over the Coals

When William Penn invited Europeans to settle in his "woods" and promised the sort of freedom that most had never known or even dreamed of, they accepted. English Quakers, Scotch-Irish and Germans were the first to cross the Atlantic and step off the ships onto what they believed was the proverbial land of milk and honey. And in many ways, Pennsylvania fulfilled their hopes. The earth was rich and fertile, the fruit trees heavy with succulent offerings and there were more than enough game and fish to feed their families. Additionally, due to William Penn's fair and just treatment of the Native Americans, white settlers lived in peace with the Lenni-Lenape.

As more people arrived, they decided to settle beyond Philadelphia and the local counties, moving west and up into the mountains. Living in colonial America wasn't easy by any means, but the colonists' hearts were filled with hope and they were willing to work hard in this new home that held such promise for them.

Philip Ginder was one of them. A German immigrant, Ginder settled on Sharp Mountain (Mauch Chunk) and built his family a log cabin in the forest. But after this, the story gets a little confusing. One account relates that Ginder's family lived on the game he shot as a backwoods hunter. There came a year when the game became sparse. Ginder was on his way home one rainy evening, empty-handed, worrying that his family would starve because his hunting expedition had failed, and he stumbled on a large black rock. Upon inspection of the boulder, he suspected it might be the hard coal he had heard about from Native American stories.

In this account, Ginder took a portion of the coal directly to Fort Allen to Colonel Jacob Weiss, who in turn took it to Philadelphia to be inspected by three men—John Nicholson, the comptroller general of Pennsylvania; Michael Hillegas, the former treasurer of the United States; and a printer

Coal mined from the anthracite region of Pennsylvania. *Courtesy of Hillmann-Purcell collection.*

named Charles Cist, who was Weiss's brother-in-law. When they wanted to see the precise location in which Ginder found the coal, the backwoodsman first asked for help in filing forms through the patent office to obtain a small tract of land to build a mill.

In another story it is suggested that Philip Ginder was actually a prosperous farmer and already a millwright when he found the anthracite. He took it to a blacksmith, who put it in a fire, and they discovered that it burned hotter and longer than bituminous coal or wood.[9] Ginder then went to Weiss with the discovery, knowing that the influential Weiss could expedite the forms through the patent office. In the end, and much to Ginder's dismay, it took so many years before he received his tract of land in 1797 that he was too old to clear it, and he sold it for 150 pounds of gold and silver.[10]

Although both historical accounts name Ginder as the person who discovered the anthracite coal that would contribute to the Industrial Revolution, the fact is that Native Americans in Pennsylvania had been using coal for many years for different purposes. A historian from a Moravian mission wrote about tobacco pipe heads that the Native Americans made from "black stone" that was easy to carve. In the 1950s, an oil company that was excavating an area near the Susquehanna River found the floor of a prehistoric Indian site. When the Society for Pennsylvania Archeology was called in to study the site, it found anthracite nuggets that had been rubbed on stone, presumably to make paint.[11] However, it isn't clear if the Native Americans ever used coal as fuel.

By the late eighteenth century, finding ways to keep homes warm and inventing methods to advance industry—particularly iron production, which was necessary to the growing new country—was becoming a challenge. Fuel was provided by wood from the region's forests, but wood didn't burn hot for very long. Colonists heated their homes with the use of fireplaces, a method that wasn't ideal since the fires burned out quickly and a spark could cause fiery devastation. Many women and children were severely burned when their clothing caught fire in the large open hearths. Benjamin Franklin invented the cast-iron stove, which allowed people to warm their homes more efficiently and with less danger, yet the stove still required wood.

Charcoal, which was the distillation of wood to its carbon content, burned hotter and cleaner, but it was time-consuming and costly, especially for iron production. Although the woodlands of America were still dense in the 1700s, the high demand for charcoal would soon strip the forests, a problem England was experiencing for the same reason. It took the yield of approximately an acre of woodland a day to feed furnaces that produced iron.

Bituminous coal from Virginia was being shipped to Philadelphia's ports, but the British blockade during the War of 1812 drove up the price of Virginia's coal. It was clear to the colonists that finding an alternative method of heating homes and fueling furnaces for iron was becoming essential.

Anthracite coal is a metamorphic rock that is formed through the buildup and decay of plant and animal material, causing organic sedimentary rock to form. Compressed vegetation forms coal, and the longer and deeper it is buried, the higher the quality.

Anthracite is hard, with a bright black luster, and it burns without flame, smoke or odor. When burned, it gives off relatively little sulfur dioxide and provides intense heat.[12] With the discovery of anthracite coal by Philip Ginder in the mountains of Pennsylvania, the young United States had found the alternative source of heat it needed, and the Industrial Revolution in America was launched.

The Lehigh Coal Mine Company

After Ginder brought the piece of coal he had found to Jacob Weiss, the group who inspected it—Hillegas, Cist and Nicholson—formed the Lehigh Coal Mine Company (LCMC) on February 21, 1792.[13] With the incentive of a money-back guarantee, fourteen people took stock in the new LCMC. The board elected Nicholson as president; then it set rules and appointed

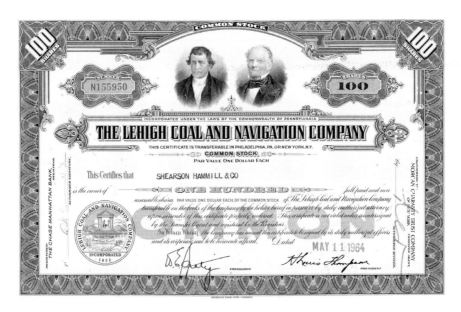

This Lehigh Coal and Navigation Company stock certificate shows the images of Josiah White and Erskine Hazard. *Courtesy of Pennsylvania Canal Society Collection, National Canal Museum, Easton, PA.*

committees to decide how to proceed with the mines. The LCMC acquired ten thousand acres of land, arranged for a road to be built from the mines to the Lehigh River and built a landing on the river. It also made arrangements to have the river improved for transporting the coal. All of this was more expensive than had been anticipated and necessitated the selling of more shares of stock. The LCMC set the price of coal at eighteen to twenty-one shillings per bushel at Allentown, Bethlehem and Easton, and twenty-one to twenty-six per bushel in Philadelphia.

In 1794, the company officially began production, with orders to transfer the coal to the Lehigh Valley by raft or flat-bottomed boat. But its progress faltered and the success it anticipated was not realized. Due to the expense of trying to improve its mines, the road and the river, the LCMC had to ask for a thirty-dollar levy on shares, and that levy resulted in delinquency by John Nicholson, Robert Morris and a number of other stockholders. The company could no longer afford to expend money on finding ways to improve the Lehigh River.

Transporting the coal over the treacherous and unpredictable waters of the Lehigh River proved even more difficult than the LCMC had imagined. Several attempts to clear the Lehigh had failed. Unable to incorporate, and with its stockholders suffering financial setbacks, the company was failing. There was a demand for anthracite during the War of 1812, and the company continued to float the coal downriver whenever it was navigable, but not with financial success. Coal was continuously lost on the twisting and wild river, and the company couldn't turn a profit. In 1818, the property was leased to Josiah White, Erskine Hazard and George F.A. Hauto, entrepreneurs of the Lehigh Navigation Company.

The Genius of Josiah White

Josiah White was the "idea man" of the nineteenth century, and his ideas led to ventures that were sometimes successful and sometimes failures. The implementation of his inventions may have failed from time to time, but the concepts were usually found to be solid.

Born in Mount Holly, New Jersey, in 1781, Josiah White and his three bothers were reared by their mother, Rebecca, after the death of their father, John White, a storekeeper and mill owner. Both his grandfather and father were steadfast Quakers who wouldn't even sell cotton in their store since it was made through slave labor. The elder White, also named Josiah, was a leader in the community who owned a tavern, kept school for Quaker families and was an apothecary, tending to the ill with local plants and herbs. Upon the death of John, Rebecca ran the mill and store, but she found that she was always struggling to support her sons. There was very little money for education, and the boys needed to work as soon as they were old enough.

When he was fifteen years old, Josiah was apprenticed in a hardware store in Philadelphia. By the age of seventeen, he was in complete charge of the store, priced the goods and kept the books. By twenty-one, he owned his own hardware store and made himself a promise: by age thirty he would be worth $40,000.[14]

He married Catherine Ridgeway, who died only two years later at the age of twenty. His sadness at her death overshadowed the fact that he had surpassed his financial goal even before the age of thirty, and he sold the hardware business to his younger brother, Joseph, and a friend, Samuel Lippincott. Josiah traveled for a while and lived a quiet, solitary life until he met and married his second wife, Elizabeth. They established their home in Philadelphia, and then Josiah purchased some property on both sides of the Schuylkill River that was located near the falls and included water power rights to the river at the falls.

Josiah, tired of being "retired" at the age of twenty-nine, invested his fortune and borrowed another $20,000 to build the first dam on the

Schuylkill and lease the water power to mills in Philadelphia. It was eighty feet long and seventeen feet wide, and instead of building the walls against the current, he constructed them to lean with the current, thereby lowering the water pressure on the dam.

It functioned well and stood strong against the annual ice floes, but the commercial rental of the water power and the collection of tolls didn't cover the expenses of the improvements. A father of one little girl now, with a second child on the way, he worried about his financial security and started a nail mill that had two purposes: it would provide income for the family and would prove that his water power was valuable. His invention of a machine that rolled and molded iron into nails caught the attention of Ebenezer Hazard, the first postmaster general of the United States and the founder of the Insurance Company of North America.

Hazard believed that the United States needed to attain economic independence from England and Europe through its own development of industrial power, and he was greatly impressed with the young inventor. He introduced Josiah to his son, Erskine, and this would be the beginning of a lifelong partnership and friendship.

Erskine was Princeton educated, and his intelligence matched Josiah's. Together they built the nail factory and a wire factory, with a patent for both the nail-making machinery and a wire-rolling machine. They were determined to convince the commonwealth and the government that water power and water navigation would prove to be important to the growth of the country. In a letter published in the *Democratic Press*, Josiah wrote, "Machinery is powerful. By using machines driven by waterpower, a single individual can do the work of at least three."[15]

Josiah and Erskine became acquainted with anthracite coal during the War of 1812, when supplies of British and Virginia coal were cut off. They purchased the "Lehigh coal" when it arrived in Philadelphia on arks, and because of their inexperience with the hard-to-ignite anthracite, they worked for hours one night trying to make a fire in the furnace. Frustrated, they and their millworkers slammed the furnace doors closed and left the mill. One of the workers had forgotten his jacket, and when he went back to get it, he was surprised to find the door of the mill was hot to the touch. Inside, the furnace was glowing.

Josiah and Erskine called the workers back and produced more parcels of nails with one fire than they ever had with the softer bituminous coal. Not certain if it was more an accident than an actuality, they used the anthracite again with the same result. Savvy businessmen that they were, they recognized an opportunity and decided to lease a coal mine so that they would have ready access to the anthracite. They also proposed that a canal on the Schuylkill River would provide a better means of transporting the coal. Erskine's father wrote legislation to authorize the improvement of the river, designating the company the Schuylkill Navigation Company, but unfortunately Josiah had made enemies because of the tolls he had charged after the first improvements he had made on the Schuylkill. Eventually the company was approved, but only on the proviso that Josiah had nothing to do with it.

In 1815, the factory was severely damaged by a fire, and Josiah and Erskine were forced to take on another partner, Joseph Gillingham, who provided the finances they needed to repair the buildings. Gillingham became disenchanted, however, when there were more problems and setbacks than profits.

Josiah and Erskine continued to move forward despite the problems they faced. When their original bridge across the falls collapsed, they built a wire suspension bridge for pedestrians that is believed to be the first wire suspension bridge in the world.[16] They then moved on to the Lehigh coal mine prospective. Josiah visited the area with his additional new partner, George Hauto, a man who presented himself as being well connected with wealthy Americans and Europeans.

At this time, the Lehigh Coal Mine Company was almost dormant, and White, Hazard and Hauto leased the property for "one ear of corn a year, if demanded by the LCMC."[17] They knew there was a great deal of work ahead of them before they could make the venture a success. First, the rough road from the mines, along which wagons had difficulty moving the coal over the mountain to the river, had to be repaired. Then, even more problematic, there were still many improvements that needed to be made on the Lehigh.

They purchased more land to improve the road. Then the Pennsylvania legislature in effect gave them the entire river on the proviso that they would complete the improvements. The authority was extensive, but so were the risks. In the legislative act, they were given authority to do just about anything they wanted to make improvements, providing they start the work on the lower part, from Easton to Mauch Chunk, within two years and finish within seven. This gave them the land and the river—but they didn't know where the money would come from to follow through when Hauto proved not to be an effective fundraiser.

Finding that some investors felt more comfortable with the mining aspect and others with the transportation piece, they formed two separate companies: the Lehigh Coal Company and the Lehigh Navigation Company. Most investors held stock in both, but not equally. Many seemed to prefer the navigation company, since Josiah had a proven track record in improving waterways and because improvements in the river would be valuable even if the coal mining failed. No one had much confidence in the partners' ability to fix the mountain road.

They raised the money they needed, set up camp and went to work on the river first. Josiah White wrote in his journal:

> *We began our work on the River with thirteen hands at the mouth of Nesquehoning Creek, the dividing point between the Upper and Lower sections of our planned Navigation. Later we rigged some scows fourteen feet wide by thirty five feet long for the eating and lodging of our then seventy hands. Another scow was rigged as kitchen and bake house. We called the fleet "Whitestown on Lehigh." It was our design to make the river navigable with small wing dams and channel walls, so as we moved from one site to another we carried all with us, until our season ended when winter froze us still in the ice.*[18]

Working side by side with his employees, sometimes waist deep in the river, Josiah devised a series of dams that had a central section that collapsed, creating what came to be called "bear trap" locks (because whenever curious onlookers asked what the engineers were working on, they were told "bear traps"). By turning a lever that opened a valve, the water escaped through the gates of the lock—or artificial dam—and raised the water in the next section, and the boat or ark could continue on to the next segment (called a sluice). These dams were durable and capable of handling large tonnage.

With the Lehigh River improvements made, the two companies were joined and became the Lehigh Coal and Navigation (LC&N) Company. The company delivered 364 tons of anthracite to Philadelphia in 1820.

The First Railroad

To correct the issues with the road, Josiah White, together with his best friend and partner, Erskine Hazard, conceived of and designed the first gravity railroad. Coal cars were placed on rails and lowered by gravity from the mines to the river, which was nine miles away. Mules were then used to draw the empty cars back up to the mines. To conserve the animals' energy, they were put on specially built cars that carried them down the mountain along with the coal and, in order to save time, they were fed on those cars. Many years later, Josiah's nephew claimed that the "Switchback Railroad," as it was called, wasn't only the first railroad, but had the first dining car as well.[19]

Josiah White's Switchback Railroad was used to bring coal from the mines to the awaiting coal boats, and it became one of America's premier attractions and its first "roller coaster." *Courtesy of Pennsylvania Canal Society Collection, National Canal Museum, Easton, PA.*

Josiah's plans became the model for future railroad construction. He designed the rails of wood with an iron plate rail, and the track was bound by crossties. It would be easy and inexpensive to build and easy to repair. Twelve miles of tracks were laid over a period of four months, supplemented by four miles of branch roads to the different mine entrances.

The gravity railroad quickly became a tourist attraction, and the company decided to allow a local businessman to run "pleasure carriages" during the off times. He charged a toll of fifty cents to strangers, twenty-five cents to Mauch Chunk residents and all LC&N employees could ride for free. Approximately 50 percent of the profits were given back to the company. And so Josiah White's first railroad also became the country's first roller coaster.

With an elevation of 664 feet and 2,322 feet long, it offered spectacular views from the top of Mount Pisgah of the Lehigh River and the mountains surrounding it. It was so popular that special excursions from New York and New Jersey brought people to see it and experience the thrill of what could easily be called a "runaway train ride." It wasn't until 1884 that an amusement park roller coaster was created and introduced to American society at Coney Island in Brooklyn, New York. Until that time, Mauch Chunk's Switchback Railroad was the only one of its kind.

Mauch Chunk (now called Jim Thorpe) became a wealthy town as more people came to work in the mines and on the arks that brought the coal to major markets. The company erected 120 dwellings and buildings, including a hotel, a store, a schoolhouse and two iron furnaces. There was one tavern—governed by strict rules and controlled by the company (which had a strong Quaker influence). Even the physician was an employee of the company.

During the years that Josiah was involved in the establishment of the LC&N, the improvements of the river and the building of the gravity railroad, he spent many long months away from his family. Elizabeth had given birth to five children: Josiah Jr. (who died at the age of five of yellow fever), John, Rebecca, Solomon and Hannah, all of whom stayed with their mother in Philadelphia while Josiah worked in Mauch Chunk. In letters written by him and to him, collected in *Josiah White: Quaker Entrepreneur* by Norris Hansell, we are able to take a peek into what this brilliant man thought and felt, and it is clear that despite his many accomplishments and bitter disappointments, he took great comfort in his relationship with his family and dearly loved his wife and children.

When old enough, Josiah's son Solomon became an apprentice in the LC&N. Josiah was very pleased and wrote to his wife:

I find Solomon useful here. I have no doubt his service here will be of as much use to him as any he might experience in another situation. Now is the time for him to learn. I trust he is in his place.[20]

Sadly, Solomon took ill when he was nineteen and died. Josiah pulled back from his work and affairs in the Lehigh Coal and Navigation Company, except in times of necessity. For a man who wrote many letters and kept a constant journal, it wasn't until three years later that he even mentioned the passing of his beloved son. In a letter to his wife in 1834, he talked about his inspection of the mines and Room Run, where his son had spent the last few months before his death.

It is pleasing to see folks here and things do look so natural here. It would all be wholly pleasant were it not for past recollections, which these circumstances so keenly revive. Our bright prospects have been cut off by an infinite wisdom which does not err.

I trust he in his innocence has passed to a better condition than if he had stayed with us and fulfilled any expectations.

Therefore our loss is his gain.[21]

In his later years, Josiah White, always a deeply religious and committed Quaker, turned to his faith, and with many of his inventions proven worthy and his industrial endeavors running smoothly, he committed his life for the greater good. He was a prolific writer and began devotional exercises that are remarkable in their beauty and illustration of faith. When informed about a devastating flood on the Lehigh River during October 1841 that took out most of the Lehigh Navigation Canal, Josiah wrote in his devotional exercises:

O Lord, help me to feel, as it in very deed is the truth, that all worketh together for good that cometh from thy unerring hand, and this affliction I know is from thy hand. Oh, let me beg of Thee to permit this apparent misfortune to drive me close to Thee as the only rock of safety, as the only sure abiding-place against all storms and all disappointments; and above all things to seek peace in Thee.[22]

Josiah was a great believer in the value of education and was always bothered by his own lack of formal schooling. An abolitionist, he believed that it was as important to educate ex-slaves in literacy and trade as it was to free them. This opinion extended to Native Americans and underprivileged children in general. He devised a plan for schools based on three important principles: 1) manual labor, "to keep the body healthy and allow a liking for productive labor"; 2) literary education, "to emphasize the useful over the ornamental"; and 3) spiritual education, "as it may make possible that a person will be a more valuable citizen of the world."[23] He implored the Indiana Yearly Meeting (a Quaker community) to take a role in establishing two schools, one in Indiana and the other one in Iowa, which they did.

Josiah White died on November 15, 1850, at the age of seventy. His wife, daughters, son-in-law and nephew John J. White carried out his instructions, especially those involving the two schools. At the time of his death, his daughter Hannah wrote, "One of our boldest champions of right order was removed by death leaving a delicate family to mourn his loss."[24]

His closest friend and confidant, Erskine Hazard, remained the manager of the Lehigh Coal and Navigation Company.

The Brawn of the Lehigh Mines

Anyone familiar with working in the coal mines understands what author Zane Grey meant when he wrote, "Writing was like digging coal. I sweat blood."

They started before dawn, moving from the dark of the early morning to the dark of the tunnels that brought them into the bowels of the earth. All of them were dressed in overalls and rubber boots and wore caps on their heads. And when the day was over, they left the mines to return home, as black as the coal they mined. Most of them were immigrants. They came from Ireland, Scotland, Italy, Hungary, Poland and Germany. Before 1842, there were no labor laws and no unions to protect them.

Miners and their families lived in what were called Patch Villages. These villages were laid out by class of mine workers, with the mine bosses and supervisors living at the head of the streets in larger, more comfortable houses. The miners' cabins weren't much more than matchstick houses, with two rooms, a kitchen area down and a garret upstairs where children slept. These cabins did little to keep out the rain and cold. The unskilled workers slept in worse conditions, in shacks sometimes filled with so many people that they had to sleep in shifts. And they paid a fairly high rent for this housing, which was taken out of their pay.

Although this book is about the Delaware Division Canal, it is important to touch on the story of the miners when talking about the transportation of the coal after it was dug out of the mountains. The narratives are intertwined, for without the first there would not have been the need for the latter; and possibly, without the brave men and little boys who descended sometimes more than a thousand feet deep into the ground with picks and shovels, the Industrial Revolution would not have been possible. It was best said by a coal miner in 1874:

> [M]*illions of firesides of rich and poor must be supplied by our labor…the magnificent steamer that ploughs the ocean, rivers and lakes, the locomotive, whose shrill whistle echoes and re-echoes from Maine to California, the rolling mills, the cotton mills, the flour mills, the world's entire machinery, is moved, propelled by our labor.*[25]

The youngest of the miners were the "breaker boys"—children who worked in the building where coal was broken and sorted. They were as young as five years old, and according to Susan Campbell Bartoletti's book, *Growing Up in Coal County*, their hours at work were possibly the hardest and definitely the most heartbreaking.

The breaker boys sat in chutes below where cars filled with coal were tipped and the contents poured into a machine that pushed the coal down toward the boys. As the coal tumbled down the chutes, a blanket of black coal dust covered the children. They wore handkerchiefs over their mouths to try to keep from breathing in the dust and chewed tobacco to keep their mouths moist. (Again, these are children as young as five years old!) They worked from seven in the morning until six or six-thirty at night with very few breaks, separating slate and rock from the coal, hunched over their work all day without backrests to give them support. They weren't permitted to wear gloves because it interfered with their sense of touch and their fingers swelled and bled until they hardened with calluses.

The breaker bosses oversaw the little boys' work, usually with a club or broomstick against their backs if they slacked off or missed pieces of slate or rock. Sometimes, if the children resisted and protested because of the abuse, they were literally whipped back to work.

The work at the breakers was no less dangerous than the work going on below ground. Children's fingers were amputated in the conveyors; others fell down the chutes and became buried in coal or fell into the crusher where the coal was being ground along with their little bodies.

In John Spargo's exposé, *The Bitter Cry of the Children*, he describes the atmosphere of the breaker:

> *Within the breaker there was blackness, clouds of deadly dust enfolded everything, the harsh, grinding roar of the machinery and the ceaseless rushing of coal through the chutes filled the ears…I was covered from head to foot with coal dust, and for many hours afterwards I was expectorating some of the small particles of anthracite I had swallowed.*[26]

Boys as young as five years old worked in the breakers, one of the most hazardous jobs in the mines. *Courtesy of Robin G. Lightly, Mineral Resources program manager, Bureau of Mining and Reclamation, PA Department of Environmental Protection.*

As they got older they were "promoted" to work inside the mines, in the damp, cold, dark and rat-infested underground chambers. But that was okay—they longed for the day. Bartoletti quotes a miner named Joseph Miliauskas, who reflected on what it was like to work as a breaker boy: "When I got down into the mines, that was paradise."[27]

"Nippers" were the youngest, around eleven years of age, and they tended the heavy wooden doors in the gangways. They were usually the first to hear the creaks and groans that would alert them to the danger of collapse, and it was their responsibility to warn the others.

"Spraggers" controlled the speed of the mine cars as they rolled down the slope—again one of the most dangerous jobs in the mines since they could be run over by the fast-moving cars when they reached down to apply the breaks. These boys lost arms, legs and their lives.

Miners descended into the dark, dank mines before dawn each morning. *Courtesy of Robin G. Lightly, Mineral Resources program manager, Bureau of Mining and Reclamation, PA Department of Environmental Protection.*

The mule drivers collected the coal in cars pulled by mules, and they could work as many as a six-mule team in the narrow passages of the mines. Although it wasn't the most pleasant job, it did afford them the opportunity to move about the mines from cavern to cavern, and it was one of the most sought-after jobs among the younger miners. Their responsibility was to get their cars full by quitting time, and if the work wasn't done, they stayed until it was. Miners were paid by the weight of the cars they filled, so it was important for the spraggers and the mule drivers to make certain that no coal was spilled or lost from the cars.

If they did the job right, they were promoted again and labored beside their fathers, brothers and uncles, working on the face of the walls of the

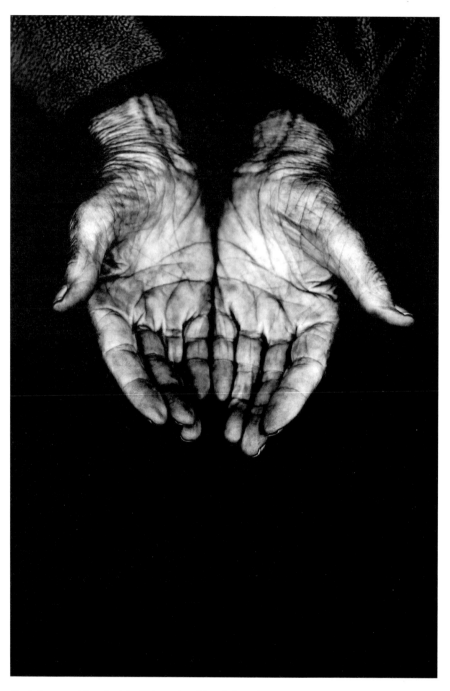

Coal dust would embed itself into the skin of the miners, sometimes permanently. *Courtesy Istockphotos.com.*

It was the backbreaking work of men and little boys in the mines that helped to fuel the Industrial Revolution. *Courtesy of Robin G. Lightly, Mineral Resources program manager, Bureau of Mining and Reclamation, PA Department of Environmental Protection.*

mountains. They shared the same risk as the men, sometimes standing for hours in dank air with water up to their ankles, knowing that at any moment the roof could collapse or poisonous gas could escape. At the end of the day, they were brought back to the surface of the earth, exhausted and covered in black coal dust that was embedded in their skin.

According to *The Death of a Great Company* by W. Julian Parton, the accident and death rate at the LC&N was consistently below the industry as a whole. "Management carried out excellent safety programs and did everything possible to train miners to work safely." Yet mining was extremely dangerous, even under the best of conditions, and miners who were not injured or killed on the job often developed black lung disease.

It is not unfair to say that the Pennsylvania miners of the eighteenth century are among the true heroes of the Industrial Revolution.

The Molly Maguires

Working conditions in the early years of the anthracite mines were indisputably hard and often brutal. Whenever men work under cruel conditions for long enough, rebellion follows. Sometimes revolt comes in the form of union activities, sometimes in criminal activity—oftentimes, both, and from both sides of the argument.

In the 1700s and early 1800s, the miners were primarily Irish immigrants. Back in Ireland, in response to what the Irish farmers believed were unfair practices by landlords, a clandestine organization called the Molly Maguires was formed to correct transgressions. How the organization got its name has always been more folk tale than factual. One story is that "Molly" was a widow who had been evicted from her house and inspired defenders; another is that Molly was a young woman who led men on nighttime raids; and still another was that Molly owned a tavern where the secret society met. Some say that the name came about because the men in the secret society disguised themselves as women when on their raids.

Philadelphians will find it interesting that in this last assumption, the Molly Maguires took on a form of the Irish practice of "mummery." (During festivals, men would blacken their faces, wear women's clothing and walk door-to-door demanding food, money or drink as payment for a performance.)[28]

In the coal region of Pennsylvania, a society of miners organized themselves in the same manner to intimidate the coal mine owners and bosses who they believed were abusing them and their sons in the mines. They tried to unionize legally and called strikes, but failed. They believed that seeking to present their grievances through the courts was a waste of time since judges, lawyers and policemen—who were mostly Welsh, German and English—deliberately caused delays and injustices because of their strong anti-Irish, anti-Catholic sentiments. As the miners became more frustrated, the Mollys' activities became more violent, and the coal mine owners answered the violence in like manner.

One Pinkerton agent, an Irish immigrant named James McParlan, went undercover in the Molly Maguires to spy on them. Based on his reports, and for the most part solely on his hearsay and testimony, twenty men were arrested and ten sent to the gallows.

There isn't much written about the Molly Maguires' activities in Mauch Chunk, except that four men were convicted and hanged there in June

1877. They were convicted of killing two mine bosses. A Carbon County judge, Judge John P. Lavelle, later described the trial in this way:

> *The Molly Maguire trials were a surrender of state sovereignty. A private corporation initiated the investigation through a private detective agency. A private police force arrested the alleged defenders, and private attorneys for the coal companies prosecuted them. The state provided only the courtroom and the gallows.*[29]

On the day of the hangings, miners and their families gathered at the scaffold and stood in complete silence to show their support of the convicted men. Security was very high for these executions. The wife of one of the men who was to be hanged arrived just after the gates had closed, and despite the fact that she collapsed in sobs, begging to be allowed in, the guards would not allow it.

No one knows for certain which of these men were truly guilty and which were "guilty by association." Chances are good that both are true.

One of the men hanged in Mauch Chunk that day was Alexander Campbell, a hotel owner and liquor distributor. He avowed his innocence throughout his trial. Campbell left his handprint on the wall of cell number seventeen in Mauch Chunk jail as he was being led to the gallows. He said that the handprint would remain forever as "proof of his words. That mark of mine will never be wiped out. It will remain forever to shame the county for hanging an innocent man." After 130 years, the handprint still remains on the wall of the cell. According to several accounts, the wall has been painted over numerous times, yet the handprint reappears. To dispel the myth once and for all, the wall was torn down and rebuilt in 1920. When the sheriff went in to look at the new wall the next day, he was shocked to find the handprint had reappeared.

The Slow Burn

With other mines being opened and operated in the mountains of Pennsylvania and privately owned waterways being built to transport that coal, the Lehigh Coal and Navigation Company needed to be competitive.

After making the transportation of coal more practical on the Lehigh River, they had to convince the general public—especially Philadelphia society—to purchase it. They knew that once the prominent families of Philadelphia started using anthracite coal regularly, the rest of the region would follow.

Anthracite coal was difficult to ignite and was inefficient as fuel in conventional fireplaces and stoves that had been designed to burn wood. Josiah White and Erskine Hazard began a public relations campaign to convince consumers that anthracite would save them money in the long run. It burned longer, hotter and without smoke. But people needed to have the correct stoves to use the anthracite effectively or the marketing campaign would not be successful.

In 1800, Oliver Evans received a patent for an anthracite stove, but it didn't take off as expected. Before White, Hazard and Hauto took over the Lehigh mining concern, Jacob Cist, facing the same predicament, had designed an anthracite stove simply by converting a Franklin stove. Cist had provided the stove and coal to several prominent families to gain testimonials. It was moderately successful; still, it was difficult to market to the average consumer.

Josiah White sent anthracite to Eliphalet Nott in Schenectady, New York, one of the country's leading combustion experts and stove manufacturers at that time. Nott worked for several years to design an anthracite stove, but didn't file the patent until 1826, which was followed by eleven patents with various improvements.[30]

In the end, the Lehigh stove was the first anthracite stove on the market, and it was cast at the Mary Ann Furnace in Bucks County by Reuben Texler.

In 1825, Walter R. Johnson, a professor who worked at the Franklin Institute, developed an air furnace for the stone coal and essentially initiated central heating for homes. Not long after heating stoves were invented, coal stoves for cooking were introduced to Americans.

With an abundance of coal being mined from the mountains and anthracite stoves in many of the homes in Philadelphia, New York and other major cities and surrounding towns, the LC&N had only one more obstacle to overcome—the Delaware River.

Chapter 3

Josiah White's Waterways

The LC&N used the Delaware River from Easton to Philadelphia, and in fact, the company's arks spent more time on the Delaware, which they didn't control, than on the Lehigh, which they did. The Delaware was more navigable than the Lehigh, yet the company was still susceptible to loss because of flooding and drought.

Josiah White decided to petition the Pennsylvania legislature to improve the Delaware and turn it into a huge canal with extensively large locks that could accommodate steam-powered ships. He brought in two men, Canvass White (no relation to Josiah) and Benjamin Wright, canal engineers who worked on the Erie Canal, to look over his plans and to inspect the work that had been done on the Lehigh. They read his proposal and were very impressed with his plans, but they admitted that they lacked the experience to help produce a canal of this grand a scheme.

Josiah's extravagant proposal met with many objections—one of which was that the Pennsylvania Assembly was already planning a transportation network across the state. Pennsylvania citizens were calling for a system of public transportation to provide access to Philadelphia, not just for the mining industry, but for timber, pig iron and other manufactured goods throughout the commonwealth. In 1825, the legislature established the first official Board of Canal Commissioners, and a second act was passed in 1826 to formally initiate the construction of public canals and railroads. The act gave the commissioners power to begin construction at three points: along the Susquehanna River to the Juniata River; along the Allegheny River from Pittsburgh to the Kiskimineta River; and down the French Creek to connect with Conneaut Lake. These were called the Main Line canals and encompassed 726 miles of waterways, associated railways and inclined plains.

Not ready to give up, Josiah and Erskine offered to construct the Delaware Division Canal at the expense of their company and not charge tolls, but again they were rejected.

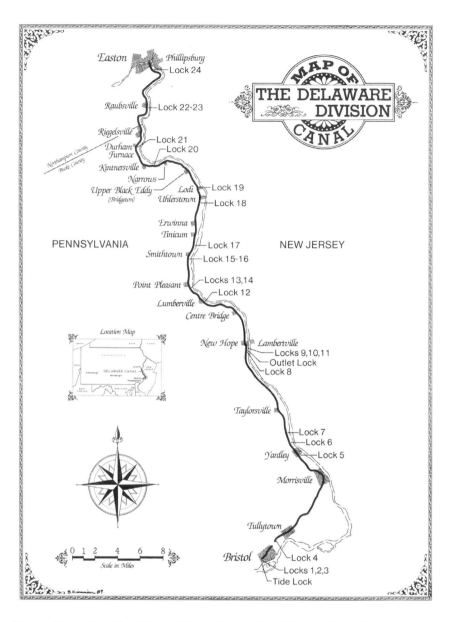

Courtesy of Pennsylvania Canal Society Collection, National Canal Museum, Easton, PA.

In April 1827, the state decided to build a small canal along the Delaware that would be part of the Main Line canal system. It would be built in the Erie Canal style and would measure 11 feet wide. The canal would link Easton with Bristol at a length of sixty miles and have twenty-four lift locks to correct the 180-foot elevation differential.

As a result, Josiah and Erskine began construction on a less imposing canal along the Lehigh than they had originally wanted to build, although it was still larger than the plans drawn up for the Delaware Division Canal. The Lehigh Canal would be wide enough to accommodate two boats passing each other. It was to be sixty feet wide and five feet deep, and because it was more conventional, Canvass White agreed to oversee the building of the Lehigh Canal. It utilized a series of slack water pools (meaning that boats would leave the canal to go into the river), with a total of forty-four lift locks, five guard locks, three guard lifts, nine dams and several aqueducts over the forty-six miles of navigation.

The Delaware Division Canal, which would run from Bristol to Easton, where it would connect with the Lehigh Navigation Canal, was started a few months after the Lehigh Navigation construction began, and although it was launched with great excitement in Bristol, the preliminary construction of the Delaware Division was essentially a disaster from the beginning.

First, there were confrontations about where the terminus should be located. Bucks County was a rural and agricultural region just north of Philadelphia. Bucks Countians knew that wherever the terminus of the canal would be located, prosperity would follow. The residents who lived in Tullytown believed that Scott's Creek would be the best spot for the canal's connection with the river and appealed to the commissioners. Bristol residents argued that, as it had been a major port since the seventeenth century and the depth of the water in Bristol was sufficient to float vessels carrying five hundred tons (as opposed to two hundred in Scott's Creek), locating the terminus in Bristol made more sense. The commissioners agreed.

Contractors needed to be hired. In their contract, the Board of Canal Commissioners required that the contractor furnish all the tools as well as the men, and a portion of his payment would be withheld until the work was approved. Contracts went to the lowest bidders, not always the best and most reliable.

On October 27, 1827, Bristol was ready to celebrate the turning of the first blade of earth in construction of the canal with great pomp and circumstance. William T. Swift, who had been appointed the grand marshal, marched five hundred men to the spot that would become Lock Number 3 for a prayer by the local Episcopal priest, followed by an address by Peter A. Brown, a prominent member of the Philadelphia bar.

Two men, George Harrison and Peter Ihire, appeared with a pick and shovel and a wheelbarrow. In a symbolic ceremony, Ihire began to dig a trench and throw the dirt in the wheelbarrow, while Harrison wheeled it a short distance away and dumped the dirt in a heap. Swift congratulated the citizens of Bucks County in yet another speech, and the band played "Hail Columbia," followed by a deafening three cheers by the attendees.[31] The crowd then went to the Delaware House, which was owned by Charles Bessonett, to continue the celebration—an appropriate venue considering that it was and still is the oldest continuously operated establishment in Bucks County, although it is now called the King George II.

Thomas G. Kennedy was the superintendent of construction and awarded contracts to dig the canal to David Dorrance and Richard Morris of Bristol for the first eighteen miles, from Bristol to Yardleyville (now Yardley). The canal was built primarily by Irish immigrants, who were for the most part unskilled. Local farmers also hired out to dig sections of the canal. The work was very difficult. Their tools were pickaxes, shovels and wheelbarrows, and the laborers were paid between forty to seventy-five cents a day, no matter how many hours they worked. These wages were

After groundbreaking for the Delaware Division Canal in Bristol, a celebration took place in the Delaware House—the oldest continuously run tavern in Bucks County, now called the King George II. *Author's collection.*

occasionally supplemented with a bottle of whiskey as a bonus. If they were strong enough and willing to do the work, they were paid extra for digging out tree stumps. At twenty-five cents a tree stump, a hardworking, capable digger could make as much as five to twelve dollars a day. The laborers had the reputation of drinking hard, fighting hard and working hard. They endured bad housing and food and long hours of work. During the construction of the canal, many men died or were killed in accidents. The summer months brought Asiatic cholera, which erupted violently and could kill within days, taking the lives of many laborers, who were quickly replaced by new immigrants waiting for jobs.

Skilled artisans built locks, aqueducts, dams, waste weirs, towpath bridges and weighing locks.

Unlike the privately built and owned Lehigh Navigation Canal, which had Josiah White and the men hired by the LC&N to work under him, the state didn't have as much access to, or they chose not to hire, truly qualified engineers. To be fair, engineers were few and far between in this country since none of the schools offered engineering except West Point. Building canals in this country involved new technology, especially the design of the locks and aqueducts, and as a result, completion of the Delaware Canal took longer than expected.

Faulty workmanship and errors in design continuously interfered with the construction and opening of the canal. In 1830, it was declared complete,

The canal was built with picks, shovels and wheelbarrows predominantly by Irish immigrants and local farmers. It required constant maintenance, which was usually conducted in winter months. *Courtesy of Pennsylvania Canal Society Collection, National Canal Museum, Easton, PA.*

but the locks were too small for the boats and there wasn't sufficient water supply to fill the waterway to capacity. Eager to have the Delaware Canal completed because not having access to the lower canal was costing the LC&N huge sums of money, the company tried to help by damming the Lehigh where it met with the Delaware, creating a pool of water to feed the Delaware Canal. Unfortunately, the canal was so badly constructed that when the water entered, it leaked dry and the canal had to be closed.

Desperate, the state turned to Josiah White in 1831 and requested that he take over the reconstruction of the canal. The longer it took to complete the Delaware, the more money the LC&N lost, so although he was still mourning the death of his son, White agreed to come out of semiretirement and act as chief engineer.[32] He went to work immediately. In a letter he wrote to John Carey Jr., the superintendent of the Upper Division of the Delaware Canal, he left no doubt about the speed with which he wanted to complete the major repairs that were needed.

> *I have just received a letter from the Commissioners directing us to make any and all repairs in situations as breaks and leaks, without waiting for specific orders, and with all possible dispatch. As Rocky Falls is the heaviest job in thy section, I particularly wish thee to proceed there with a strong force and get it to hold water.*[33]

And in another letter to the Pennsylvania Board of Canal Commissioners, it is clear that he is disgusted by the way the canal was built in the first place.

> *I have advised the Board, and wish to proceed with certain changes in the water wheels and fixtures for supply of the canal with water below New Hope. Please inform me by early mail whether I am to direct the work to be executed according to the earlier design or whether I am to have the liberty to make such modifications as I may deem best for the purpose intended...All my experience has gone to prove the impolicy of multiplying machinery when it is not absolutely necessary.*[34]

Although there is no mention of it in any of his letters, White must have been infuriated by the fact that had the state allowed him to build the canal when he requested, it would have been completed earlier and correctly. He spent time and energy repairing the canal, addressing the inconsistencies in the locks and aqueducts and trying to fire the men who were not doing their jobs effectively.

By 1832, under the direction of Josiah White, the Delaware Division Canal was repaired properly and was open for use. It was one of the first sections of the state public works to be completed and, in the long run, perhaps one of the best built. The *Easton Whig* reported in November 1833, "The Delaware Canal is in the full tide of successful experiment and the Lehigh Canal is stout and strong."[35]

The work Josiah supervised corrected the leakage problem, and the Lehigh was feeding the upper canal properly, but the engineers building the waterway found it necessary to introduce other feeders of water into the canal for the lower level. One of the most industrious and unique was the use of a lifting wheel located at the Union Paper Mills, just south of New Hope, which raised water from a wing dam into the canal. It was built by Lewis S. Coryell and, except for one overhaul in 1880, this water wheel continued to feed the canal without trouble throughout the life of the canal. There were essentially two wheels. The outside wheel was built with paddles that were turned by the flow of water. This controlled the inside wheel, which caught the water in trough-like buckets and emptied into a sluiceway under the mill and into the canal on the other side. The canal was now fully watered.

There were about twenty creeks that flowed directly into the Delaware Canal channel, but they couldn't be counted on to contribute water to the canal. They did, however, deposit large amounts of silt into the channel during spring thaws and heavy storms, creating more work for

A water wheel built at the Union Mills just outside of New Hope helped to water the lower end of the Delaware Canal. The mills have been turned into upscale condominiums with beautiful views of the Delaware River. *Courtesy of the Historic Langhorne Association.*

Tolls were collected at the tide lock in Bristol and again in New Hope. Industrial buildings and mills were built along the edge of the canal, as seen in the background. *Courtesy of the Pennsylvania Canal Society Collection, National Canal Museum, Easton, PA.*

the maintenance crews who used shovels and wheelbarrows to remove it. Maintenance on the canal was constant, with quick fixes taking place in the summer months and larger problems solved during the winter months.

At its completion, the Delaware Division Canal was sixty feet long, forty feet wide and seven feet deep. The entire system cost $1,400,000 to build, with additional funds expended in maintaining the canal. There were constant repairs due to leaks, floods and freshets. It was initially believed that the Pennsylvania state canals could be built on borrowed money, and once in operation the loans would be paid off and there would be a surplus paid into the treasury. But when it was completed and a crowd of coal-loaded boats could be seen floating up and down the waterways, the prosperity residents expected wasn't forthcoming. They were exceptionally outraged when taxes were raised to pay the debt.

The revenue from tolls barely exceeded operating expenses. As a result, the state-owned canals were sold to private concerns. In 1866, a ninety-nine-year lease agreement was made between the Delaware Division Canal Company and the Lehigh Coal and Navigation Company.

Chapter 4

Locks and Their Keepers

Locks, Aqueducts and Waste Weirs

Locks were crucial to canal operation. They kept the canal water at an even level to allow boats to travel both upstream and downstream no matter the elevation and with no damage to the cargo or the boat. Along the length of the Delaware Canal, there was a gradual drop of 164 feet that necessitated twenty-four locks along the canal.

Built like boxes, locks were set into the canal with gates at either end. The locks built on the Delaware Division were eleven feet wide and ninety-five feet in length. Although initially designed to be built of wood, the Board of Canal Commissioners ultimately were convinced that there was enough stone in the region to build the locks with stone, and the additional costs would be made up in the lack of maintenance later on. A "doghouse" beside the lock contained the mechanisms that would control the opening and closing of the gates as the boats approached and left the locks. A wicket gate was located at the downstream end of the lock, and the fall gates—or drop gates—were upstream where the water pressure was constant. When a boat entered the lock, the gates were shut behind it. Then a valve opened and allowed water to flow into the chamber. The boat rose with the water (or fell, depending upon which way it was moving on the canal) and once the water level matched the level in the next section of the lock and was at a proper depth for the draft of the boat, the gate opened and the captain motioned to the mule driver to begin pulling the boat through so it could continue on to the next section of the canal.

Both company-owned boats and privately owned boats were weighed empty at the start of each season. Then, at the beginning of every journey on the canal, once they were loaded with coal in Mauch Chunk, they would be led into a weigh lock. When a boat was secured inside the weigh lock, the water would lower until the boat rested on the cradle of a large scale.

Gates at Lock 20 in Kitnersville. *Courtesy of Historic Langhorne Association.*

The weighing gear was located inside a building next to the lock where the tender would make notations of its weight in a log beside the LC&N number or name of the boat. He would then hand the boat captain a slip with that information—the weight of the load, the time and the charges.

Canalboats could carry up to one hundred tons of coal, and each captain of a company boat was allowed two hundred pounds extra per trip for his own use to sell, trade for food or goods along the canal trip or save for the winter.

There were several types of locks along the canal. Some kept the boats moving down to Bristol and others changed the boats' direction across the Delaware River to the Delaware and Raritan Canal. Some of the locks along the Delaware Canal were large enough for two boats to enter at the same time; these were preferred by the boatmen, as they saved time.

When boats were headed to New Jersey to continue their trip on the Raritan Canal, they crossed the Delaware at Lock Number 9 in New Hope. The lock tender would raise a red flag so the New Jersey tenders would know that a boat was ready to cross. The boat would enter what was called a feeder lock to await the crossing. Here, the weight of the boat was measured with the use of a rod that estimated the draft of the boat in the water, and again that data was entered into a log.

Most of the locks on the Delaware Division Canal were built of stone. This lock in New Hope, which is now empty, shows the stone from local quarries that was used in construction. *Author's collection.*

Lock 11 in New Hope as it looks today. Until flooding in the fall and winter of 2007, the canal and locks were fully watered and operational up to Centre Bridge. Repairs are expected to be complete in late 2008. *Author's collection.*

Crossing the river from New Hope to New Jersey required skill and precision. There were specially trained workers on the New Jersey side who would take a flat-bottomed boat across the Delaware from Lambertville, and while doing so would gauge the speed of the river's current, its depth and how the weather would affect the crossing. If the river was low, some of the boat's load was transferred to an empty scow to adjust the draft of the boat. The scow would be attached to the boat or brought over separately. When the workers reached the boat waiting to cross, they tied a rope to the stern of the boat and attached the rope to a winch connected to a cable that was secured to a tower upstream from the outlet lock. With a long-handled bar placed into a hole in the winch, the men would tighten the rope to draw the boat carefully out of the lock and into an eddy, holding it steady against the current. One end of the line from the pulley was secured to the bow of the boat and the other end hooked to the side. By adjusting the length of the rope attached to the side of the boat, the pilots could change the angle of the boat to accommodate its speed and ensure the safest passage across the current. Controlling the speed of the boat was extremely important. A boat that crossed too quickly could jam or damage the outlet gates, requiring costly and time-consuming repairs.

There were four locks in New Hope, including an outlet lock that allowed cargo boats to cable across to the New Jersey side of the river. *Courtesy of the New Hope Historical Society.*

Once on the New Jersey side, the boats were hooked up to mules again, which pulled them through the locks to the Raritan feeder and then proceeded down the Raritan Canal to New Brunswick. From there the boats moved on to New York.

There were nine aqueducts on the Delaware Canal that conveyed the canal over streams and depressions in the ground below the bottom of the canal. They were made of wood at first and the ends rested on stone masonry built into the canal. The aqueducts were usually the same depth as the canal, 20 feet wide and ranged in length from 25 to 178 feet. The towpaths were connected on each side of an aqueduct by a wooden platform. Where smaller streams that didn't require aqueducts were located, culverts were installed so that the water could flow beneath. There were twenty culverts in total, and they consisted of arched masonry or large tubes.

Controlling the level of the water in the canal was tantamount to its safety and that of the boats. In addition to feeding water into the canal by several methods when it was running dry, it was equally important to lower the water when it was too high.

Tohicken Aqueduct. *Courtesy of Historic Langhorne Association.*

When the water rose slightly above normal level, it was controlled automatically through overflows, which were reinforced depressions that directed the overflowing water into lower ground beyond the canal bank. If the water rose to a dangerous level, special gates at the top of a waste weir were opened to allow the water to escape from the canal. These were also used to drain the canal between locks when maintenance or repairs were required. In order to regulate the height of the water in the canal, stop gates were also installed at certain points. They were normally open, but could be closed quickly in the event of a flood. There were nineteen waste weirs and eight stop gates on the Delaware Canal.

Considering that time was money for the boatmen, going through locks efficiently, controlling the water and crossing the Delaware were of great concern, and sometimes caused serious distress. The faster the boats moved through the locks the better, and when it took longer than they wanted, the lock keeper received the brunt of the boatmen's wrath. Not that the lock tenders worried too much—they could easily exact revenge on an offending captain since they were in complete control of the passage on the canal.

The Keepers of the Locks

The canal system in Pennsylvania spurred economic growth in a new and expanding country and provided employment for boat builders, boatmen, manufacturers, agricultural suppliers, merchants and others (even prostitutes) who earned their living in the canal industry. Thousands of Americans, as well as immigrants, found employment in canal construction, maintenance and operation.

When the construction of the Delaware Canal was nearing the end, lock keepers were appointed by the canal commissioners. Several of them had participated in building the canal, and some were local residents. According to the *Delaware Canal Journal* by C.P. "Bill" Yoder, the following men had been assigned as the first lock tenders on the Delaware Division Canal:

John I Hibbs would work at Lock Number 1 and the Tide Lock at Bristol
Elias Gilkyson was assigned locks 2 and 3 (Bristol)
Daniel Kirgen was on 4 (Tullytown)
Charles Shoemaker, 5 (Yardley)
Joseph Suber, 6 (located between Yardley and Taylorsville)
David Kirgen, 7 (North of Yardley)
Samuel Daniels oversaw 8 and 9 and the Guard Lock at New Hope
Samuel Stockdan worked locks 10 and 11 (New Hope)
John Everitt, 12 (Lumberville)
George Solliday, 13 and 14 (Point Pleasant)
Mahlon Smith, 15 and 16 (Smithtown)
John Speer, 17 (just south of Tinicum)
Ralph Harrison, 18 (Uhlerstown)
George Fox, 19 (Lodi)
Wyllys Rogers, 20 (Kintnersville)
Charles Wagener, 21 (Durham Furnace)
and Joseph Shepherd, 22 and 23 (Raubsville)
Lock 24 at Easton did not have an assigned locktender right away.

In the early years of the canal, the locks were open all day and all night. Around 1855, this changed, and the lock tenders worked from four o'clock in the morning until they closed the locks at ten at night, six days a week. During the height of the canal age, the boatmen kept the lock tenders very busy. At the peak of operations on the canal in the mid-1800s, as many as between twenty-seven hundred and three thousand boats were logged at the tollhouse at Bristol. Boats could make as many as twenty-five to twenty-eight round trips throughout the operating months from mid-March to mid-December.

Most of the homes in which the lock keepers and their families lived were owned by the company. They were usually very tiny, of saltbox design and

A good lock keeper would start to fill the lift lock as soon as he heard the sound of the boatman's conch shell so the boat could lock through quickly and continue on its way. *Courtesy of the Historic Langhorne Association.*

made of fieldstone or wood, sometimes with no more than two rooms on the first floor and a loft for sleeping above. Many of the lock tenders farmed the land around the homes and kept goats, chickens and other livestock in order to feed their families.

When they heard the call of the conch shell that the boatmen used to notify the lock tenders of their approach, they would respond with their own whistles or horns. Three blasts meant hold your position; one meant it was clear for the boat to approach. Once they were adept at figuring out from which direction the sound of the conch shell had come, efficient lock keepers would be certain to have the lock filled with water even before seeing the boat approach. It wasn't unusual for there to be several boats in line waiting to pass through a lock, especially at single locks, and the boatmen were very impatient. Occasionally they tried to pass the boat in front of them to get to the lock first, causing arguments that often erupted into fistfights. According to the Bucks County Historical Society, "Fights took place nearly every day at the locks and at the tie-up places."[36]

Lock tenders kept order at the locks, or at least tried to. The Board of Canal Commissioners had set in place official regulations that the canal men were expected to respect, and they were fined when they violated those laws. Bickering and brawling were violations, and heavy fines were doled out to captains who failed to yield the right of way. There were rules as to which boats went through a lock first. Any boat arriving within one hundred yards of a lock would be allowed to pass first. When lock keepers felt that boatmen were flagrantly disregarding the rules of lockage, they would report the violators to the canal boss, who in turn would catch up to the offenders and administer a stiff fine.

It was also the lock tender's responsibility to keep the overflow control gates set and make certain that the sluiceways were clean and working. Depending upon where their locks were located, they may have been in charge of the waste gate. The company relied on them to report damages or leaks and, when possible, make repairs. They took care of their lock houses and the land on which the houses were located. They even hunted muskrats, which burrowed into the banks of the canal and caused some of the worst damage, often as much as $5,000 worth of damage. For all of this, the lock keepers were paid $4 a day and given free housing by the company.

They were expected to live by rules just as the canal men were, and they could lose their employment if reported by a canal boss for violations. They could be fired for being found drunk while working (and they worked just about all the time) or if they were away from the lock tender house for more than a week, regardless of whether they had someone else working the locks. They couldn't disturb their neighbors and, for the most part, were expected to respect the boatmen and not cause trouble with them or among them.

Some lock tenders' children learned how to operate the gates at a young age. Mechanisms were protected in a "doghouse" similar to this one. *Courtesy of the Pennsylvania Canal Society Collection, National Canal Museum, Easton, PA.*

Appointments of lock tenders were political, and being given the job of moving into a suspended lock tender's house depended upon which political party was holding the reins at the time. There were some who were well liked and kept their jobs until their deaths, and even after their deaths their wives and children were permitted to carry on.

To make extra money during the canal season, some of the lock tenders' wives took in the boatmen's laundry, baked breads and pies to sell to them and occasionally ran stores where the boatmen could purchase supplies and food. There were lock tenders who worked second jobs or farmed the land, so they trained their wives and children in the mechanics of operating the locks while they were away from their stations. Lock tenders normally worked on the maintenance and repair of the canal during the winter months, and they cut ice when the canal and river froze over and sold it to the icehouses. And there were times when it was their unfortunate job to help fish a dead mule or a human body out of the dark waters of the canal.

A young boy named James Lair was found dead in the canal one morning near the Yardley lock. He had been at the tiller the night before and the pilot was below in the cabin sleeping. When the captain realized that the boat had run aground, he raced up on deck to find the fourteen-year-old boy missing. They found him before noon with a gash on his face. They suspected that the boy nodded off, and as the boat moved under one of the bridges, he hit his head on the support, was knocked off the boat and drowned when the mules continued to pull the boat.[37]

That was only one of several incidences in which a young boy or a man was found dead either in or beside the canal. In the November 1907 *Bucks County Gazette*, an article titled "Found Dead in a Canal Basin" reported:

The body of Joseph Larrisey, of Bristol, was found early Tuesday morning in the small basin which is formed by the canal overflow in the lot between the railroad and the canal…William P. Brink, the tender of No. 3 lock, at about 7:30 in the morning was attracted to the spot by noticing a derby hat on the bank of the basin and after going over to investigate saw the head of a man submerged in the shallow water.

And in an article printed on November 23, 1852, a sad report was published:

Morris Masten, aged about fourteen years, son of John Masten of Plumstead, was drowned in the Canal, eighteen miles above Easton, on the 28th ult [sic]. He fell off a Canal Boat unnoticed, and when discovered, he was beyond the reach of assistance in time to save his life. His remains

were brought to his father's residence, and thence carried to the Plumstead
Mennonite burying ground and interred on the Sunday following.[38]

Once the boats passed all of the locks on the canal and reached Bristol, they went through an outlet lock in the Delaware River and were towed by steam tugs to Philadelphia. The Lehigh Coal and Navigation Company owned three side-wheel steamboats, which towed the canalboats to Philadelphia and other tide points. They could pull twenty boats in strings of three side by side. Then they would come back to Bristol and start up the canal on their way back to Easton.

The locks are no longer in use and the lock tenders' houses, what is left of them, are privately owned; yet some of the lock keepers left a part of themselves behind in different ways. In the *Bristol Pilot*, published on September 17, 1998, in an article titled "Delaware Canal Brought a Growing Business to Bristol," Paul Ferguson of the Bristol Cultural and Historical Foundation is quoted as saying:

> *At the first lock there was Abel VanZant. He operated lock one with his wife Mary. Mary had children. Every time VanZant had children he would plant a black willow tree. Today we can see thirteen black willow trees which we presume are descended from the willows.*[39]

Bristol was the final stop on the boatmen's journey before turning around to ascend the canal. The basin is located behind the children in this image. *Courtesy of the Pennsylvania Canal Society Collection, National Canal Museum, Easton, PA.*

The locks in New Hope were the halfway point between Easton and Bristol. *Courtesy of the New Hope Historical Society.*

Even years after the end of the canal age, the Delaware Division Canal has taken lives. Several young children have meandered away from their backyards along the canal and slipped under its idle waters. A businessman from York, Pennsylvania, took a wrong turn in his car and drowned in the canal. In October 1983, well-known NBC television news anchor Jessica Savitch was having dinner with a close friend, Martin Fischbein, the president of the *New York Post*, at Chez Odette's in New Hope—a historic tavern that was a popular boatmen's stop. It was raining when they left the restaurant. Savitch's dog, Chewy, was in the car with them when they took a wrong turn from the parking lot and drove along the towpath rather than on the road. The car veered left, went over the edge and turned upside down in the shallow water of the canal. The station wagon sank into the mud, sealing the doors shut. Savitch, Fischbein and the dog were trapped inside as water poured into the car. All three drowned.

Chapter 5

Beside the Busy Canal

The building of the Delaware Canal introduced opportunities for other businesses, and industrious Bucks Countians could make an ample living beside the waterway. Numerous businesses emerged near the canal—taverns, hotels, stores and stables for the mules. Mule trading and stabling became lucrative businesses, as did boatyards, quarries and mills.

From Bristol to Easton, taverns at canal level provided an evening's respite from the boredom of the mule-drawn trip from lock to lock. Tavern fare back then was hardy, if not fancy. Meals varied according to the season, but the most commonly served were ham, bacon, beefsteak and fowl. Breads were a staple, of course, as were fruit pies and apple butter. Eggs, butter and cheese were all served, along with a varied selection of vegetables that included potatoes, carrots, peas, beans, beets, onions and cabbage. And for those places that weren't influenced by the temperance movement in the 1800s, a supply of beer, applejack, whiskey, rum, gin and even brandy was available.

Canalboats had a wet well but no proper refrigeration to keep food fresh. As a result, stores along the canal provided necessities for the boatmen and their mules. Perishable foods were bought daily, and many of the local residents made a living supplying the boatmen with fresh-baked bread, cheese and meat.

Expenses round trip from Mauch Chunk to Philadelphia could cost three dollars, which included feed for the mules. Bacon cost four cents per pound; ham, six cents; butter, twelve cents; coffee—which was a boatman's staple—twelve cents; and brown sugar, four cents. They also purchased baskets of potatoes and bushels of oats.

It is said that during the temperance movement no liquor was sold in stores along the canals, but Francis Rapp reports in "Lehigh and Delaware Canal Notes" that a drink called "strap" was sold at the locks and canal stores, and from the reputation of the canallers, liquor must have been

In addition to being an "avenue of commerce," the canal also provided water for fire trucks in the later days of the canal era. This photo was taken near Lock 11 in New Hope. *Courtesy of New Hope Historical Society*

available somewhere along the way, for the boatmen were always ready to "throw one back."

> *Strong drink served to break the monotony for the men, and, it can be assumed, increased the tendency to crime. Abundant apple jack and black strap made with rum and molasses were available at every basin, dock, and even the locks. There were also floating saloons and plenty of taverns along the canal route. Saloons offered free stabling for the mules and lewd women to lure the boatmen off the water.*[40]

Perhaps that is how "Devil's Half-Acre" in the township of Upper Black Eddy got its name. Now known as Point Pleasant, the majority of development in Upper Black Eddy was centered on the canal. There were stables for the mules, a shipyard and a general store. A tavern was built in the 1800s while the canal was being constructed. The owner ran the tavern illegally and was often in trouble with the authorities and with the rough-and-ready canal men who found comfort in bottles of whiskey and the arms of "ladies of the night." There is a legend that the area where this tavern was located is haunted by the ghosts of canal workers who were buried in shallow graves after being killed in drunken brawls.[41]

Taverns, Stores and Stables

Merchants catered to the canallers in Bristol, where the basin was located, and in almost all cases the stores extended credit to the boatmen. This was where they stocked up at the beginning of their return trip. And in Bristol there was no shortage of taverns and inns. Most canal men enjoyed a beverage and meal at the Closson House (formerly the Delaware House), where they could await orders for their return while their coal loads were transferred to steamers. At the waterfront below this saloon, fifty or more canalboats could be seen docked while the men prepared for the return.

Bristol was always bustling with canallers and their trade, and more often than not, they brought unwanted trouble with them. In Doran Green's *History of Bristol Borough*, he relates how stimulating life with the canallers in town could be.

> *One day a well-known young man with several companions was playing a game of cards on one of the canal boats. A row occurred and when the young man's body was found next day, from marks upon his head, he was supposed to have been murdered by being struck by some hard instrument. Great excitement prevailed throughout the town. Several arrests were made, but no incriminating evidence could be found and the matter remains a mystery to this day.*[42]

If they *survived* their stay in Bristol, the canal men boarded their "light" boats and headed back up the canal. It was a day's trip from Bristol to Yardley, and they usually tied up for the night and stabled their horses there. The Continental Hotel and the White Swan (now the Yardley Inn) were the stopping points at the Yardley lock. Both places are still popular establishments today. During recent renovations at the Continental Hotel, a secret room was found in the lower level of the building that confirmed the legend that the Continental had once hidden escaping slaves from the South.

In Yardley (then called Yardleyville), there was a store on Edgewater Avenue that sat along the towpath. The owner of the store, a Mrs. Reed, would go down to the canal to see what the boatmen needed and then bring their orders to them; this was especially helpful if the captain wasn't stopping in town and wanted to move on to the next lock before nightfall.

Between the major towns, some of the residents along the canal would offer provisions—baked bread and produce—and the LC&N made arrangements for mules to be stabled in barns along the way. Where the canal ran parallel to the river with just the towpath between them, bridges

This page: Homes located on the canal often accommodated the boatmen with food, drink and stabling for their mules. This home was originally built in 1740 and was licensed as Beaumont's Tavern. Because of its proximity to the canal and the remnants of a bridge nearby, it is likely that it stabled mules for the night and offered provisions to the canallers. *Courtesy of Jim and Tina Greenwood.*

were provided so that the mule drivers could unhitch their teams and lead them across the bridge to the stables.

Once the canallers arrived in New Hope, they had their choice of spots to imbibe. Originally called Coryell's Ferry, the village was a major encampment during the Revolution, and in the years following the war, development in the village grew when merchant Benjamin Parry made it his home and built his Hope Mills there. When the mills burned down, he rebuilt and renamed them New Hope Mills, and eventually the town adopted the name. The building of the Delaware Division Canal helped to establish New Hope as a central district. Four locks were located in the borough, including an outlet lock to the New Jersey side of the river connecting to the Raritan and Delaware Canal.

The River House, which was built in 1794, was a favorite stop for the boatmen. After the canal years, it became known as Chez Odette's (owned by a French actress who starred in movies and onstage and who made her home in New Hope), but three major floods in the early 2000s finally closed this famous restaurant.

A rather popular brothel called the Bucket of Blood was always accommodating to the canallers who were so inclined to accept hospitality there. Although the renowned Logan Inn is located on the canal, it was a hotel for more sophisticated tastes and pocketbooks, and boatmen rarely, if ever, slept off their boats. Established in 1722 by John Wells, the founder of New Hope, the Logan Inn is one of the oldest continuously run taverns in Bucks County and is listed in the National Register of Historic Places. During the Revolutionary War, George Washington stayed at the Logan numerous times, and during the summer of 1777, General Benedict Arnold headquartered there—before he became a notorious traitor. Since New Hope was the halfway mark between Easton and Bristol, the boatmen restocked many of their supplies there. The Defiance Cigar Store and T.E. Watson's provided cigars and chewing tobacco, and in the borough close to the canal there were livery stables, a harness maker, a foundry, a flax factory, a fishery, a shoemaker, a milliner, a lumber merchant and four doctors. A good deal of mule trading took place in New Hope as well.

Once they were north of New Hope, the boatmen passed through several small communities that, before the appearance of the canal, had been sleepy little villages. One of them was Centre Bridge, a charming village connected from Pennsylvania to New Jersey in 1814 by a suspension bridge. There is no lock for the canal at Centre Bridge and so it was not a regular meeting place of canal men, as they rarely stopped between locks. But the area was a favorite of some of the American impressionists who set up studios and purchased homes in the picturesque surroundings. The Centre Bridge Inn is entwined with the history of the canal simply because of its proximity, and when the present owners, Tina and Jerry Horan, purchased the Centre Bridge Inn, they were given a lease to run the New Hope Canal Boat Company, which provides interpretive boat rides for passengers between Centre Bridge and New Hope. Drawn by mule teams—Dot, Dolly, Joe and Daffodil—these rides include a boat captain who explains what life along the canal was like in the nineteenth and early twentieth centuries. When not being used for interpretive presentations, the boats convey small private parties from the restaurant to give passengers a feel for what it was like when the canal was used for recreational purposes on Sundays. Not unlike many of the establishments along the Delaware River that have been hit hard by recent floods, the Horans have worked nonstop in partnership with the Delaware Canal State Park to keep the canal repaired and maintained.

Located about one and a half miles north of Centre Bridge was a place called the Cake and Beer House, where boatmen stopped for the night, stabled their mules and ate.

The Centre Bridge Inn continues to offer respite to weary travelers—inside and on canal barges built and operated to keep the history of the canal alive. *Courtesy of Center Bridge Inn and New Hope Canal Boat Company.*

The Black Bass Hotel (once called the Lumberville House) was also famous for feeding and accommodating canal men, along with lumbermen who worked in the mills there. Lumberville was founded by Colonel George Wall, an officer in the Continental army, and even before the Delaware Canal was built, Lumberville was a thriving locale due to the abundance of fine trees—white pine, spruce, hemlock, oak, beech and chestnut—used for shipbuilding and houses. In the early days, the logs were cut, hauled to the river and floated down to Philadelphia from Lumberville. When mills were established to cut the wood for easier transportation and sale, the lumber was loaded on boats and brought to its destination by the canal. Because of the town's proximity to the river, some of the original businesses located along the main river road had to be eliminated to make room for the canal, and the doors of houses that fronted the river were relocated to the back of their homes in order to gain access to the redirected road.[43]

The LC&N stored blasting powder and other supplies at the Black Bass, which almost resulted in a tragedy when the hotel caught fire one night. If it had not been for the courage of the owner, Major Anthony Fry, who ran into the burning building to remove the explosives, it would have been blown to pieces along with some of the town. Today, despite the many floods it has endured, this establishment is a renowned bed-and-breakfast, hosting guests from all over the world.

Jacob Oberacker ran an establishment called the Delaware House in Erwinna, and it became one of the canallers' favorite stops. Oberacker provided a change of mules, beer, salt cakes (similar to soft pretzels) and a bed for the night. Today it is called the Golden Pheasant Inn and is on the National Registry of Historic Places. Its owners, Barbara and Michel Faure, continue to serve travelers in this charming bed-and-breakfast. Sitting on the outdoor terrace overlooking the canal, it is easy to envision what it was like during the height of the canal era.

Benjamin Riegel founded a town and built a tavern along the Delaware Canal in 1838. Soon after, Canal Street in Riegelsville became one of the largest industrial manufacturing centers in America, dotted with mills and factories, including a paper mill owned by the Riegel family. Mansions were built on its hillsides, and the town remained prosperous well into the twentieth century. It is still one of the most charming towns along the canal.

Many communities sprung up along the canal simply to supply provisions for the important waterway, and with the demise of the canal, many of them faded away again. Shipbuilders closed their doors, taverns closed down and stables weren't needed any longer. Except for two or three, the stores in which boatmen and locals gathered around the stove to exchange

Boatmen stopping at Jacob Oberacker's would be served salt cakes similar to our soft pretzels. Today, this favorite stop of the canallers is called the Golden Pheasant and is owned by Michel and Barbara Faure. *Courtesy of the Golden Pheasant Inn, Erwinna, PA.*

The barroom at the Golden Pheasant, then called the Delaware House, served boatmen during the height of the canal age. *Courtesy of the Golden Pheasant Inn, Erwinna, PA.*

gossip, argue politics and complain about the LC&N are gone. Sadly, most of the covered bridges along the canal were washed away by floods.

However, several suspension bridges that cross over the canal and the river remain, as do many of the charming camelback bridges. Bridges in Washington's Crossing, New Hope, Centre Bridge and Riegelsville are all open to pedestrians and offer beautiful views of the river and canal.

Keeping soap on the boat was a problem for the canallers because when the soap was wet, it often slipped from a person's hands, plopped into the canal from the deck of the boat and sank into the silt and mud at the bottom of the canal, never to be seen again. Losing brown soap to the bottom of the canal was a common complaint of the boatmen.

The owner of the store on the Morris Canal in 1891 decided to stock a new brand of soap that was white. He believed that the new Proctor & Gamble product, Ivory soap, might be easier for the boatmen to see at the bottom of the canal and they would be able to fish it out with a scoop.

A canal captain bought a bar of the white soap from the merchant and decided to use it right away. As anticipated, the fresh bar of soap slipped out of his hands and into the canal. Annoyed that he was about to lose a brand-new bar of soap, he grabbed the scoop immediately and rushed to the side of the boat to see if he could find it before it sank all the way to the bottom. Much to his surprise, he found the cake of soap floating beside the boat. He scooped it up, amazed and delighted with his new floating soap.

He was so impressed, in fact, that he was quick to share his discovery of the new soap with every boatman he passed. He spread the news of the floating soap up and down the canal and in Phillipsburg and Mauch Chunk when he was filling up his boat with coal. Soon, all the canal men who had access to the store that carried Ivory soap bought several cakes to keep on their boats.

A representative of Proctor & Gamble was curious when he saw the huge amounts of soap the store proprietor was selling, and he visited the store to inquire as to why the soap was selling so well there. The proprietor informed the representative that the canal men discovered "Ivory soap, it floats." And so began the slogan for Ivory soap.[44] Or at least that's one story. Another, less amusing, is that Harley Proctor, after a chemist listed the ingredients in percentages, wrote the slogan "99–44/100ths Percent Pure: It Floats." The canal store owner's story is more fun.

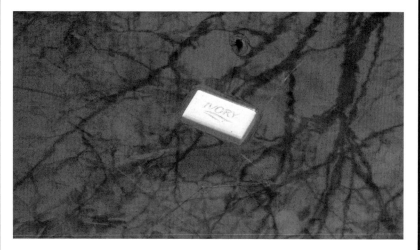

Ivory soap was the choice of the canallers when they discovered it floated instead of sinking to the bottom of the canal. *Author's collection.*

Chapter 6

Snappers and Stiff Boats

Early Travel on the Delaware

Aside from the canoes of the Native Americans who were the first inhabitants living along its shores, the first boats on record that traveled on the graceful 360-mile river that separates Pennsylvania from New Jersey and parts of New York were captained by Europeans. European exploration in the region began with Henry Hudson in 1609, followed by Adrian Block of the Netherlands and, in 1610, English Captain Samuel Argall, who named the watercourse after Lord De La Warr, governor of Virginia.

In his search for the Northwest Passage in the Americas, independent explorer Captain Thomas Yong of England sailed up the Delaware River as far as the falls, near what is now called Morrisville. Captain Yong spent time exploring the fertile river valley and making friends with the Lenni-Lenape, who were the first inhabitants in the region. His Native American friends told him of great mountains beyond the falls—the same mountains that would provide anthracite coal and feed the Industrial Revolution 150 years later—and in a report to King Charles, he promised to find a way to move beyond the falls and explore farther up the river. His promise was never to be kept because he left the Delaware Valley to continue exploration on the Hudson River and did not return.

When William Penn first arrived in America and staked out the land that was granted to him by King Charles II, his mode of transportation from Philadelphia was by boat. He was greatly impressed with the area he called "Buckinghamshire," where his country home, Pennsbury Manor, was built. It took five hours for visitors to Pennsbury Manor to travel back and forth from Philadelphia by river, and the unpredictable currents could make it a difficult trip. Yet, because of the lack of decent roadways, the Delaware was the easiest way to travel locally.

The time it took to travel on the Delaware by a boat similar to William Penn's depended upon the wind and the strength of the men who were onboard to row when there was no breeze. Homesteads—also called plantations—along the Delaware in colonial days provided stone docks along the river so that boats could stop to discharge passengers in safety.

Ferries were established to provide crossings between New Jersey and Pennsylvania. Colonists wanted accessible water supplies for their settlements, and many of the sales from William Penn's earliest records show that immigrants purchased tracts of land along the rivers, streams and feeder creeks first. Later purchasers chose tracts between streams. Major waterways were used to transport produce and manufactured goods to Philadelphia and New Jersey, and so boats, canoes and barges were found cluttered along the shores of the Delaware. A Pennsylvania law was enacted in March 1771 that declared:

> When the improvement of the navigation of rivers is of great benefit to commerce, and whereas many persons have subscribed large sums of money for this purpose…the Delaware and Lehigh Rivers shall be common highways for the purpose of Navigation.[45]

Eventually, sawmills sprouted up in the dense hardwood forests of the countryside, and the trees were cut along the Delaware and floated down to the city, at first individually and then tied together to make rafts.

> The first raft consisted of six pine trees, or logs, 70 feet long and to be used for masts for ships then building at Philadelphia. A hole was cut through the end of each log and the logs strung on a pole, called a "spindle," with a pin through each end of the pole outside the logs, to prevent them spreading apart.[46]

The travel of log rafts through the numerous falls and rifts was extremely dangerous. Raftsmen took their lives in their hands every time they embarked down the river anywhere north of Philadelphia. Dangers along the Delaware included Foul Rift above Easton, an obstacle course of falls a mile below New Hope called Wells Falls, the Scudder's Falls and a nine-foot fall over a length of thirty-five hundred feet at Trenton Falls, all of which were major impediments in navigating the river.

According to W.W. Davis's *History of Bucks County*, two men, Mr. Skinner and Mr. Parks, successfully navigated the first raft to Philadelphia over the falls, and upon arriving in Philadelphia unscathed, Skinner and Parks were heralded as heroes. Mr. Skinner, who was the "captain" of the raft, was

Durham boats were first used to transport cargo on the Delaware River before the canal was built. General George Washington used these boats to cross the Delaware on that infamous Christmas night before the Battle of Trenton. *Courtesy of the Washington Crossing Historic Park, administered by the Pennsylvania Historical and Museum Commission.*

called "Lord-High-Admiral of the Delaware" until his death.[47] The height of river rafting was between 1835 and 1850. In 1873, there were reportedly thirty-eight mills at twenty-three locations between Easton and Morrisville.

Work boats, like this shovel dredge, kept the canal waters at a safe depth. Maintenance on the canal was ongoing throughout the season. *Courtesy of the Pennsylvania Canal Society Collection, National Canal Museum, Easton, PA.*

In the 1700s, Robert Durham designed a boat that was sturdy enough to carry iron made at the Durham Furnace to the markets in Philadelphia and beyond. These flat-bottomed boats were built with sides that were twelve to fourteen feet from the boats' ends, which tapered in to glide easily through the water. They measured approximately sixty feet long by eight feet wide and forty-two inches deep and could carry a load of seventeen tons while traveling downstream and two tons when moving upstream. In time, they were employed to carry not only pig iron and ore from the Durham Furnace and Mills, but also grain, whiskey, flour, corn and other products to and from the region. The Durham boat required a crew of at least three men to operate it, and they used twelve- to eighteen-foot "setting poles" to steer the boat going downstream and to push the boats upriver. Later models were fitted to use oars. These boats played a major role in one of the most important battles of the Revolutionary War. They were the method of transportation used by General George Washington to deliver his troops across the Delaware on Christmas night in 1776 before winning the Battle of Trenton. There are several Durham boats at Washington Crossing Historic Park on display, and they are still used in the annual reenactment of that infamous crossing every Christmas.

Arks were also built to transport goods—primarily anthracite coal—on the Delaware. Built in Mauch Chunk in 1806 by a man named William Turnbull, the first ark was loaded with three hundred bushels of coal and successfully floated down to Philadelphia, where the ark was then broken up

Boats on the canal were called snappers, stiff boats, packers, flickers, chunkers and scows, but they should never be called barges since, unlike barges, the boats on the Delaware Canal had steering mechanisms that the boatmen used with great skill. *Courtesy of Historic Langhorne Association.*

and sold for lumber. Subsequent arks were rectangular boxes 20 to 25 feet long and 16 feet wide connected by hinges so that a chain of arks, as long as 180 feet, could be assembled quickly. But transportation by ark wasn't always successful. They were easily damaged by jagged, jutting rocks along the river, and they would become stuck in low water and couldn't continue on their journey until the water in the river rose to safe levels.

Arks were costly—especially to the forests surrounding Mauch Chunk—since they could not make a return trip upriver. The five-man crew that navigated the arks downriver returned to Mauch Chunk by foot, carrying the nails and joints with them so that they could be used for new vessels. According to Michael Knies's book, *Coal on the Lehigh*, as many as thirteen men built twelve arks of six or seven sections in one week.

There were also boats called "flickers" that were used before the Delaware Canal was built. R. Francis Rapp, who built boats in Erwinna from 1858 to 1882, tells us in "Lehigh and Delaware Division Canal Notes":

> *After the Lehigh canal was built, a smaller boat, called a "Flicker" was used, these were let out of the canal at an outlet lock at Easton into the*

Delaware River and floated down as far as Bordentown, where they entered the Delaware and Raritan canal by an inlet lock and proceeded thence to New York. This could only happen at reasonably high water and was impossible at low water... These so called flicker boats were only used before the building of the Delaware Division canal, after which the present day canal boats were used and the flickers given up.[48]

Soon, a new kind of boat would become the standard for transporting goods and products to Philadelphia, one that wouldn't need to fight the currents and navigate the falls.

Canalboats

With the conversion of the Lehigh Navigation and the Delaware Division Canal into a two-way system, allowing boats to travel upstream as easily as downstream, and the decrease in lumber due to the denuded forests, the arks that were being used had to be redesigned. The new boats were constructed to fit through the many locks along both systems. The eleven-foot width of the locks on the Delaware Canal dictated that the boat be no wider than ten and a half feet.

Before long, boatyards sprouted up along the canal, from Bristol to Easton. The new boats were diverse, and they were called by different names, sometimes humorous, often after heroes and virtues—names such as *Sabbath Rest*, the *To and Fro*, *May Flour*, *Ladies Friend* and *Star of Bethlehem*. The *Molly-Polly-Chunker* was made famous in the ending years of the canal age when a group of people that included Louis Tiffany made a trip to Mauch Chunk from Bristol. There were packers (built by Asa Packer), flickers, chunkers (any boat built in Mauch Chunk), stiff boats, bullheads, scows and hinge boats, and there was even a "beer" boat. But make note: *there were no barges.* It is important that we understand, when discussing the Pennsylvania canals, that the vessels used to transport coal, lumber, ore and produce were not barges.

According to Lance Metz of the National Canal Museum:

It's an insult to the people who piloted the boats. A barge has no rudder and is simply pulled along by mules. The boats used on the Delaware Canal needed strength and skill to maneuver them and it was hard work.

They were built to withstand rugged wear and tear. Steam-bent, hand-cut, white oak planking was joined with hand-forged spikes to the ribs and framing. The boats' cargo areas contained false bottoms, with lining planks over the ribs and air space of about five inches. They were designed so that coal could be shoveled out easily and bilge water pumped out when necessary. The life of a canalboat could be twenty-five to thirty years.

The Lehigh Coal and Navigation Company boats were distinctive. Painted a deep chestnut brown called Spanish brown and trimmed with white, every company boat was marked on each side of the bow with the company logo, a large white circle with a dark center. The label "L.C. & Nav. Co. No." followed by a number assigned to that particular boat was painted across the stern. The captains of these boats were hired by the LC&N.

The company also operated mud diggers or shovel dredges that removed—or redistributed—the sediment deposited by streams and storm water so that the canal was kept at a six-foot depth in the middle. In addition, there were work scows and carpenter boats that repaired the banks and the locks.

Privately owned boats also worked the canal, and instead of being numbered, they were named by their owners, usually after wives, mothers, daughters or sweethearts. The only rule on the canal was that there would be no duplication of names.

One of the most successful men to benefit by the discovery of anthracite coal and the building of the canals on the Lehigh and Delaware was Asa Packer. Mauch Chunk had become the wealthiest town in the United States at that time. More than fifty citizens of Mauch Chunk had a personal wealth of $50,000, which is the equivalent to $1,000,000 now.

Packer, who was born in Mystic, Connecticut, in 1805, apprenticed as a carpenter to his cousin in Susquehanna County. He saw an advertisement for a coal boat captain on the Lehigh Canal and he applied. Within three years, he was assigned a second boat with his brother-in-law. His fleet grew, and he decided to return to carpentry to build coal boats and canal locks for the Upper Lehigh Canal. His boatyard produced closed-hatch, sixty-ton coal boats that were known as "packer" boats. With the profits from his boatyard, Packer purchased coal lands and soon controlled a share of the coal market. By 1850, he was the richest man in Mauch Chunk.

Additional boatyards were located in Easton, Uhlertown, Erwinna, New Hope and Bristol. Michael Uhler was a merchant who opened a general store in Allentown initially. When the store burned down and he suffered a great monetary loss, he moved to Uhlersville. He opened another store and began a limestone business after purchasing thirty acres of limestone property in Northampton County—only a half mile from Easton. He had eight large kilns to manufacture lime along the canal bank and had an annual output of 250,000 bushels.

Limestone was an important industry in the Delaware Valley. Lime was used as farm fertilizer and in masonry cement, and limewater also had uses, such as whitewashing barns, chicken houses, fences and other structures. Uhler's kilns supplied most of the farms in the region that purchased lime products. He also established a gristmill on his property that produced flour and feed.

He built and owned twenty-five of his own boats to deliver his lime along the Delaware Division, Morris and Delaware and Raritan Canals, and he built and repaired boats for others. Uhler's industries kept as many as one hundred men employed year-round. In the early twentieth century, men who worked for the boat builder earned forty cents an hour, and a foreman could make as much as fifty-eight cents an hour. At that time, it took about two hundred days to build a boat.

In "Lehigh and Delaware Division Canal Notes," Rapp proudly discusses the boats he built at his boatyard in Erwinna.

> *Canal boats are about eighty-seven feet six inches long, ten feet six inches wide, and seven feet high midship with a shear of six inches bow and stern and carry about 100 tons of coal on a load. The No. 6 built in my boatyard at Erwinna in the year 1872 was loaded at Mauch Chunk and passed the weigh lock August 12, 1872, with one hundred and twelve tons of coal to New York. This being the largest record tonnage carried by any one boat through the canals from Mauch Chunk to New York. The same boat on September 30th, in the same year, carried one hundred and ten tons to New York, making a record that has never been broken by another boat.*[49]

One of the earliest independent canalboat operations was the Red Line Transportation Company out of Easton. It was organized soon after the opening of the Delaware Division Canal in 1836, and Captain Jacob Able was the president. These boats carried general merchandise instead of coal, with capacities from sixty to eighty tons.

But it was the coal-loaded boats that took up the greater amount of the canal industry. The larger boats came in two sections, called hinge boats or "snappers," and single boats were called stiff boats. They traveled approximately thirty miles a day, two miles an hour when full and four miles an hour when empty. They required a crew of at least two people, one to steer the boat and one to drive the mules. Very often, canal men brought their whole families aboard to live and work with them during the canal season. Some of them didn't own homes except for their boats and lived on their boats even in winter when the canal was emptied for maintenance.

Boats would move nonstop from four or five o'clock in the morning until ten o'clock at night, and mule drivers took breaks by riding on their mules. They would tie their wrists to the mules' traces so they wouldn't fall off if they fell asleep. *Courtesy of the Pennsylvania Canal Society, National Canal Museum, Easton, PA.*

Every boat was equipped with a stove—sometimes two, one on deck and one in the tiny cabin below—a barrel for water, a toolbox, a night hawker (headlight) and a pole. Poles had many uses, and there were different types: a bow pole, stern pole and hook pole. The hook pole was a multipurpose tool. A steel rod was inserted on one end of the pole with a hook at the other end. It could move a boat along a wharf, push or change the location of a boat and fish things out of the canal that may have fallen off deck (sometimes even people). Time was money, and once on the move, it was very rare for a boat captain to stop the boat for anything but entry into a lock, so the hook pole was also used by the mule driver to vault to and from the towpath onto the boat when he needed to get onboard to eat or when being relieved by another driver.

In the early days of the canal, ten-plate stoves were used for cooking. Some boats had stoves made of sheet iron with a grate. Pans, coffeepots and other cooking utensils were placed on top of these stoves, which were located near the hinges. The captain of the boat would usually do the cooking.

The steersman, while cooking, had to run from the cabin, to the stove, back and forth to the rudder, and set the table on the cabin deck, while the other man or boy was on the tow-path, after which he took the tow-path and the other man came on board and ate his dinner, the boat never stopping.[50]

A capstan or windlass was a necessity on a boat. The device, shaped like a spool and usually made of wood, was mounted vertically in a bearing in the foredeck and was used to pull a boat off accumulated silt or other obstructions at the bottom or sides of the canal by turning a rope from an anchor.

On the bow of every boat hung a "night hawker," which was a lantern about twelve inches square with glass on three sides that burned kerosene. This was the headlight of the boat, and it lit the way during the dark morning hours and the blackness of late night.

The cabins in the boats were built into the stern and were accessible by a set of steps similar to a ladder. They were usually eight by ten feet and seven feet high, only large enough to hold a stove, stool, two hinged bunk beds and a hinged table. When not in use, the hinged table and bunks fell against the walls to give the cabin more floor space. In slightly larger cabins, there may have been a cupboard. Women who lived on the boats sewed curtains for the tiny windows and used tablecloths to make the cabin feel homier. Oil lamps provided light in the cabin and sometimes pictures adorned the walls.

To canal men, especially those who owned their own boats and didn't lease them from the company, their boats were the center of their lives. It was a boatman's home, his place of business and even where his children were born and sometimes died. Men as old as seventy and boys as young as sixteen could captain a boat. For many families, working the canal was a multi-generation business. For some it was all they knew. They played music, wrote poetry, traveled in the dark of early morning and late night, steered their boats under the oppressive heat of summer and shivered in the cold without protection from the elements as they steadily moved up and down the canal, stopping only when they had to. Their boats were their base—their heaven and their hell.

Chapter 7

The Mules

It has been said that boat captains' mules were almost as important to them as their children. Mules were part of the canalboat team, working as hard as the captain and mule driver—sometimes harder. Where the men and little boys slept in the tiny cabins of the boats or sometimes on deck, exposed to the elements, the mules were well taken care of and put up in the numerous stables along the canal. It cost fifteen cents to stable one mule at night, twenty-five cents for two mules, and the captains didn't hesitate to pay the price.

Because of their importance, when a mule became lame or died, the canal men had no choice but to purchase another one for their team. Mule teams would cost anywhere from $300 to $400, and the better the quality of the mules, the more the boatmen could brag. They were an investment, and because of their importance, a canal man sometimes treated them with more deference than he did his own family. Losing a mule to lameness or death cost a boatman dearly; in fact, losing a mule and having to replace it would negate the amount he would earn from a round trip hauling coal.

Half Horse, Half Donkey, All Muscle and Brains

The fact that festivals have been held across the United States strictly to honor mules is testament to their worth. In Columbia, Tennessee, they have even crowned a special mule each April as king for a day during what they call a *Mulesta*, and mules from around the countryside parade together to the courthouse, where a girl places a jeweled crown between the king's long ears.[51]

A mule's dam is a horse and his sire is a donkey, and it appears that most mules inherit the best qualities from both. He has the strength, courage and speed of the horse, and the patience, long ears and sure-footedness of the donkey. A mule has the ability to grow sleek and strong on nothing but grass. Some say he is stubborn, but most muleteers call it wisdom. If his load is too heavy, he expects the mule driver to lighten it. If he's been put to work for too long, he stops until he's rested. If the pasture in which he's eating is hilly, he eats uphill so he won't have to bend too far down. And if the weather is unbearably warm, he slows his pace—whether the human driving him likes it or not.

Horses will work themselves into exhaustion and will dash blindly over a cliff, but mules practice moderation instinctively—they don't overeat and they rest when they need to. They endure heat better, they aren't gourmet eaters—plain clean hay or grass is good enough for them—and they rarely have hoof problems, as their hooves are strong, tough, flexible and don't split or chip as a horse's will. They even live longer than most horses, and they excel in physical soundness.

Additionally, the mule is easier to breed than its counterpart, called a hinny, which is the offspring of a male horse and a female donkey. Both are almost always sterile, except in very rare cases, which is a result of the differing number of chromosomes of the two species. Donkeys have sixty-two chromosomes and horses have sixty-four.

The mule was introduced to this country when George Washington heard of the exceptional abilities of the mules that the Catalonian donkeys in Spain sired. The king of Spain was honored by President Washington's interest and sent two of his finest as a gift to the new country. One died onboard the ship during the passage, but Washington was thrilled with the other one when it was presented. "From him," President Washington said, "I hope to secure a race of extraordinary goodness which will stock the country. He is indeed a Royal Gift, and henceforward that shall be his name."[52]

Americans who saw the offspring of Royal Gift working on Washington's farm were amazed to find how durable Washington's new mules were. They wanted to breed their own mares with Royal Gift, and soon Virginia's farms were being plowed and cultivated by Royal Gift's "sons and daughters."

Owners of working animals prefer mules to horses since their skin is harder and less sensitive than horses' skin, and they show a natural resistance to disease and insects. Mules have a combination of hair types, with coarse main hair and a tail more like a horse than a donkey, and they don't have pronounced arches to their necks. Their bray is mixed with that of a horse's whinny, and they come in different sizes and shapes. There are miniature mules under thirty-six inches and others that can measure up to seventeen hands. It is interesting to note that they can also strike out with any one of their hooves and in any direction, which many canal mule drivers found out the hard way.

They are the perfect work animal. They have a strong sense of self-preservation, which is probably why they last longer than horses, and people who have worked with them for years come to heed their mule's actions.

Pets of the Mines

Mules were used extensively in the coal mines. Because of their intelligence, they knew what to do even without a mule driver leading them. When young boys were sent into the mines to handle the mules, they were told to "watch the mule and learn something."[53]

Mules were stabled underground in the mines where boys would care for them. They were rarely brought above ground after being put to work in the mines. *Courtesy of Robin G. Lightly, Mineral Resources program manager, Bureau of Mining and Reclamation, PA Department of Environmental Protection.*

The mules' compact builds were perfect for working in the narrow passageways of the mines. They lived deep in the mines, in stables that were cut out of rock and other materials located near the "cage," where the miners entered and left. Some never saw the light of day, which is disturbing considering how much they love to roll in the grass and stretch their muscles after a long day of work. Yet, the mine bosses knew that the mules were important to the productivity of the mines, and the animals were well cared for, perhaps even more so than the human workforce. The stables were cleaned out daily and the mules were combed, checked for sores and fed well on oats, corn and alfalfa.

The boys who took care of the mules usually became very close to the animals, and some of them would even ask their mothers to pack sandwiches or fruit for their mules when extra food was available. Not that it was necessary since the mules would help themselves to whatever was in the boys' lunchboxes—eggs, pork chops, bananas, bread crusts. The boys even shared plugs of tobacco with their mules, and some of the mules grew so addicted to the tobacco that they refused to work until they were given their share.[54]

According to Susan Campbell Bartoletti's book, *Growing Up in Coal County*, mineworkers came to depend on the intelligence of the mules and their good memories. Miners believed that mules knew their way through the tunnels better than anyone else did, and if they lost their way, they unharnessed the mule and allowed the animal to lead them to safety.

Their intelligence could be frustrating, however, since they knew exactly how many cars they were supposed to pull, and should a driver sneak another one on the train, the mule wouldn't budge until it was removed. It never paid for a mule driver to be mean to a mule—the animal never forgot and usually got even no matter how long it had to wait to do so. Weeks after a boy would twist a mule's ear or beat him with a stick, he could count on receiving a kick in the stomach or seat of his pants.

Four-legged Canallers

Mine mules' lives were very different from those of the boat-pulling mules, just as life was different for the boys who drove the mules along the scenic canal than for those who worked in the black, dank atmosphere of the mines. Yet close relationships developed between the humans and the mules above ground just as they did below.

The mules that walked the canal were usually better "dressed," too. Canallers would decorate their mules' harnesses with bells that jingled a melodious tune. The bells came in useful when a boat moved through dense fog—the boatman at the rudder could steer by listing to the sound of the bells. Many of the mules wore straw hats that were tied under their chins with holes cut out on the brim to make room for their ears.

Sensible boatmen looked down on others who were cruel to their mules. They knew the invaluable contribution mules made in keeping the boats moving along the canal, and a good mule team, once it was trained properly, could travel the towpath and pull a boat without a driver for long stretches between locks.

In an article in the *Bulletin*, Grant G. Emery, once a canalboat captain, told reporter Henry R. Darling:

> *A half decent mule with any brains at all was a lot better than a horse. After a couple of trips, the mules knew the canal as well as we did. They knew when to start, stop, and slow down. You didn't drive the mules. You let them go by themselves.*

Inspectors made regular rounds on the towpath to check the condition of the mules, and a captain could be arrested for improper treatment of his mule. Emery recalled in Bill Yoder's *Delaware Canal Journal*:

> *They had a woman down there, she'd make you stop the mules and lift the collar; and, if there was a sore on his shoulder, you had to take that mule out, you couldn't use him. They'd slap a fine on you. She was all through the Delaware.*[55]

Emery was referring to Eva Huston, who was the SPCA representative on the Delaware Canal at the time. Eva's concern was well-founded considering the complicated tack the boat-pulling mules had to wear, which included harnesses, fly nets in the summer and waterproof blankets to cover their backs and shoulders in stormy weather.

Of course, mules didn't always need someone else to "speak" for them when they weren't happy. Many mule drivers received a swift kick that would send them into the canal, and if the hoof hit them in the wrong place, it could mean a serious—or even fatal—injury.

Normally there would be a team of two mules, often three, and occasionally a horse would be part of the team. They were harnessed in tandem, with the lead mule in front and the second mule or horse—called the shafter—behind the lead. There was what was called a spreader, which kept the traces (lines) spread between the first and second mule to protect their legs from becoming chafed. The mule that was attached to the towline was harnessed to a cross stick called a stretcher.

The mules would work a sixteen-hour day, resting only when the boat went through a lock, and they pulled their load at a steady pace of 2 to 4 miles per hour. They made the round trip from Mauch Chunk to Bristol and back, which was 212 miles, in seven or eight days. At the end of the day, when their harnesses were removed, they would lie down in the grass and roll in great delight, twisting their necks and flexing their legs. This was their way of relaxing, and it also revived them. In fact, if a boat was close to a lock or at the end of the canal near Bristol, but the mules were showing fatigue (and when they were tired, no amount of pulling, prodding or cajoling would get them to move), boatmen would unharness the mules, allow them to roll in the grass and then hitch them up again to make the last few miles to the basin of the canal.

Although feed bags were attached to their harnesses every four hours, sometimes mules that weren't muzzled would stop along the towpath to graze. They were especially fond of eating poison ivy. And, like the mules that lived and worked in the mines, boat-pulling mules were just as fond of tobacco. If a mule driver was careless enough to leave his tobacco in his back pocket, the lead mule would pull it out with his teeth, and trying to get it back could result in a swift kick.

Boatmen stabled their mules at night in private or company-owned stables along the canal. It cost fifteen cents to stable a mule for the night; twenty-five cents for two mules. *Courtesy of Jim and Tina Greenwood.*

The New Hope Canal Boat Company, with the help of Captain Dave, mule driver Charles and mules Dot, Dolly, Joe and Daffodil, keeps canal history alive during interpretive canalboat rides in New Hope. *Author's collection.*

Mules weren't fond of water, which also made them perfect for canal work. Where a horse might decide to take a swim in the canal, the mule would back away from it. They took drinks at overflows and sometimes in the canal, but kept a safe distance.

Occasionally, and always with great chaos involved, mules would fall or be pulled into the canal. If one mule went into the canal, the other was bound to follow since their tack bound them together, and if they weren't assisted out immediately, they would drown. When it happened, the mule driver or captain would try to cut the traces as quickly as possible, because the loss of a mule—or worse, a team—meant a loss that a captain may not be able to recoup.

The great inventor and head of the Lehigh Coal and Navigation Company, Josiah White, found the intelligence of mules very interesting. As mentioned in an earlier chapter, when he completed the gravity railroad in Mauch Chunk, White decided that the mules that worked outside the mines would be carried down the mountain in specially built cars—called "wagons"—on the loaded train in order to save time. Once the coal was unloaded from the train, the mules would pull the empty cars back up to the mine. During an annual report of the Lehigh Coal and Navigation Company, White included a note about the mules. It read:

> So strong was their attachment to riding down, that in one instance, when they were sent up with the coal waggons [sic], without their mule waggons, the hands could not drive them down, and were under the necessity of drawing up their waggons for the animals to ride in.[56]

Miles of Mules

Mules are an icon of our national heritage because of the importance they played in the nation's economic development. In the summer of 2003, a public art project was launched throughout the Delaware and Lehigh National Heritage Corridor; that is, towns and villages in Bucks, Lehigh, Northampton, Carbon and Luzerne Counties. The project featured more than 170 life-sized fiberglass mules.

The Miles of Mules program in Pennsylvania was sponsored by businesses, schools, individuals, families and nonprofit organizations. A committee of fifteen volunteers in Bucks County called the "Grooming Committee" reviewed artists' applications and ideas on how they wanted to decorate a fiberglass mule. When their applications were accepted, they received a $1,000 honorarium to cover expenses.

The mules were decorated by renowned local artists, amateurs and students who worked together to decorate the mules as school projects, all of whom used unique mediums and reflected their own styles and personalities or that of the region. There were traditional mules, colorful mules and sometimes outrageous mules, and all were unique. The project pulled together extensive community and business involvement. Once decorated, the mules were put on display throughout the region in public "paddocks" all along the canal corridor.

Rosemary Tottorato, who owns a graphic arts and communications company in Newtown, created a mule she called *Mule Tales*. Using this unusual medium, she wanted to communicate the important events that

Above: During the Miles of Mules project in 2003, 175 fiberglass mules were decorated by renowned artists, amateurs and students and placed in "paddocks" throughout the Delaware and Lehigh National Heritage Corridor. *Courtesy Rosemary Tottoroto, Tutto Design and Communications.*

Right: Using old newspaper articles and narratives by canal men, Rosemary Tottoroto tells the stories of the Delaware Canal in *Mule Tales*, which she designed for the Miles of Mules project. *Courtesy Rosemary Tottoroto, Tutto Design and Communications.*

This whimsical mule decorates the gardens of the Golden Pheasant Inn in Erwinna. *Courtesy of Michel and Barbara Faure.*

Salvaged, by artists Pete and Jennifer Miller, uniquely interprets the strength of the mule and the animal's "heart of gold." *Author's collection.*

The Mules

Sitting on the banks of the now quiet canal, Jim and Tina Greenwood's mule stands in tribute to the working animals that kept the canalboats moving from four o'clock in the morning until ten o'clock at night. *Courtesy of Jim and Tina Greenwood.*

Ben was created by artist James Feehan and now lives in the garden of the lock tender's House No. 11. Surrounding *Ben* are John Thompson, Jack Thompson, Susan Taylor, Jan Wolters and Betty Orlemann. *Courtesy of the Friends of the Delaware Canal.*

took place during the canal era. "The challenge was how to do it on a life-sized fiberglass mule." She went to the National Canal Museum Archives in Easton for research, and then with two sizes of rubber stamps, Rosemary told the stories of the canallers by carefully stamping quotes and newspaper articles all over her white mule. It took her seventy-five hours to complete.

When the "Summer of the Mules" drew to an end in November 2003, "The Mane Auction Event" was held in Bucks County, and forty-five of the decorated mules were sold at auction at the Michener Museum in New Hope. The proceeds of this auction benefited the Delaware and Lehigh National Heritage Corridor, the Michener Art Museum and other nonprofit groups such as Habitat for Humanity, Big Brothers Big Sisters of Bucks County, Artists in Residence, Fox Chase Cancer Center and many more worthy organizations.

Some of the owners of the mules have been kind enough to share them by displaying the mules around Bucks County for everyone to enjoy.

Chapter 8

The Canallers

Men, women and children worked the mule-driven canalboats from early spring to early winter, stopping only when ice prevented their boats from moving on the waterway. Babies were born on the canal, and death was a shadowy companion.

But who were they? How did their life's work become a boat, a mule team and a load of coal? Some of the earliest canal workers were from local towns and villages, farmers turned boatmen. Others were free men of color. Yet the majority of the canallers were drawn from the nineteenth-century immigrant pool, primarily the newly arrived Irish, Scotch and Germans. Some had worked in the anthracite mines, decided they couldn't take that life any longer and exchanged their Davy safety lamps for night hawkers. Others had worked on the excavation of the canal channel, and when it was complete, exchanged their shovels for rudders.

Immigrants to Pennsylvania in the colonial period were mainly English, with a large population of Germans (150,000 by 1775) and Scotch-Irish (175,000 by 1775). Approximately 5 percent of the population was French, Dutch, Welsh, Swedish, Jewish, Irish or Swiss. When the American Revolution began, the population of "Penn's Woods" had grown to nearly 300,000 and was one of the largest colonies in America with the most diverse population. After the American Revolution, immigration continued at a rate of approximately 60,000 a year, mainly from Western and Northern Europe. In the early and mid-nineteenth century, those numbers increased greatly with Germans fleeing Europe because of crop failure and religious persecution, and the Irish escaping the potato famine. Between 1830 and 1860—the height of the canal age—more than 2,000,000 Irish and approximately 1,500,000 Germans arrived in America.[57] Many of these new immigrants made their way to Pennsylvania.

The German influence on both the Lehigh and Delaware Canals was very strong. In fact, on the Lehigh there were so many German canalboat

On the canal, the light boats returning to Easton had the right of way. Martha Best, whose laundry is hanging on the line of her husband's boat, steers toward the berm to allow LC&N boat 267 to pass. *Courtesy of the Pennsylvania Canal Society Collection, National Canal Museum, Easton, PA.*

captains and lock tenders that even the Irish and the African Americans who worked the canal learned the German dialect.[58]

The German Immigrants

For many years they were erroneously called "Pennsylvania Dutch," but in fact, not all German-speaking immigrants were from the Netherlands. Many were Palatine German, Alsatian, Swiss, Hessian and Huguenot, and although they were primarily Quakers, German-speaking groups of various religious affiliations—including Lutheran, Reformed, Anabaptists (Amish, Hutterites and Mennonites) and Catholics—also settled in the colonies.

The earliest German immigrants in America came to Philadelphia County during the years 1683–85, and more came in the early 1700s. They left their European homes at the invitation of William Penn, whose First Frame of Government promised religious freedom and economic growth. Penn was particularly impressed with the organized Quakers in Holland and Germany long before he was granted land from the King Charles II, and when he was establishing his colony in America, he campaigned to persuade all persons interested in economic opportunity and freedom from religious persecution to immigrate to Pennsylvania by offering five-thousand-acre tracts of land at £100 per tract.

Germantown in Philadelphia County was where most of the German-speaking immigrants settled. In 1689, William Penn signed a charter incorporating Germantown, appointing Francis Daniel Pastorius as the first bailiff. (Later, Pastorius was to draw up a written protest against African slavery in 1688; it was the first in American history.)

All immigrants shared a common method of journeying to the shores of America—they came by ship. Each voyage was unique, and some fared better than others, but there were many immigrants who did not survive. It was a common practice that when a ship approached the shore, the dead were brought off first and buried in ditches along the beach. Those who were left onboard faced the New World alone. Sometimes they were orphans; other times they were parents who had dreamed of a better life for their children but now had empty arms.

In Philadelphia, by the mid-1700s, there were sixty-five docks covering the west bank of the Delaware River, and those docks were crowded with new immigrants. When ships approached the shores of Pennsylvania, people gathered on the wharf, some to greet family members, others to find workers. Merchants were alerted by newspaper advertisements when German servants for "sale" were arriving by ship.

All the immigrant passengers disembarked and were taken to the courthouse, where they pledged an oath that they would conduct themselves as good and faithful subjects of the British Crown and that they would renounce any allegiance to the pope. They signed their names to two papers—one belonged to the king and the other to the government of Pennsylvania.[59]

Many of the new colonists who had come with money didn't remain in Philadelphia. According to settlement patterns in southeastern Pennsylvania, they flocked to the countryside where they could purchase homesteads and begin to farm their land—their *own* land—happy to have shrugged the yoke of tenant farming in their European homes. The farther away from Philadelphia, the more affordable land was. For the most part, Germans attempted to settle in pockets, since it was easier to communicate with each other and help one another when they planted their crops and built their homes.

Newly arrived Germans settled in Lancaster, Berks, Northampton, Bucks and Montgomery Counties. They walked over Native American paths through dense woods or traveled in canoes on the river and following Indian creeks to find their settlements. They brought with them skills as craftsmen and millers. They grew corn, squash and wheat in fertile soil, and they raised healthy livestock. Their barns were so well built and impressive that English settlers started to adopt their methods. And they established schools.

Before long, the Germans were holding public office. They worked diligently to establish their presence in their new country. They wanted religious freedom, a government that would allow them to control their own lives, land and success, all of which they found.

And the Germans weren't alone in these dreams. As the iron and coal industries grew in America in the 1800s and offered a greater—almost insatiable—need for laborers, an influx of immigrants came to the newly formed United States from many different countries. Fifty different nations and ethnic groups were identified among the immigrants of the nineteenth century, all longing for a better life, more opportunity and a kind of freedom they had never known.

The Pennsylvania coal mines and canals brought many of them to the Lehigh and Delaware Valleys.

The Irish

It would not have been quite as easy for the Irish immigrants to pledge an oath to renounce the pope when they were taken to the courthouse in Philadelphia, and so began their tribulations in America.

By all accounts, the boatmen were a rough bunch and had a reputation for fighting and drinking—or at least the Irish did. The fighting instinct in the Irish could be partially genetic, but in fairness, it is also a result of the kind of environment in which they lived, under the thumb of the British Crown. The Quakers and other Protestant religious sects came to America in search of freedom to worship according to their own consciences and because of the religious persecution they experienced, and so did the Irish, but for the Irish their Catholic religion was an obstacle to being accepted in the mainly Protestant colonies of America. Although Pennsylvania did allow greater religious freedom than other colonies—and in fact, the Catholic Mass was allowed first in Pennsylvania—the Irish Catholics experienced discrimination.

The Irish had been impoverished in their own country for many years. The Crown had given land grants to Protestant English citizens—land that the Irish Catholics had lived on for ages—and it caused constant hostilities. The Irish became defensive, self-protective, frustrated and very often hopeless. They fought with their Protestant landlords, and they fought among themselves about whether they wanted a free-state form of government or a republican form of government once they revolted. While they were arguing amongst themselves, they had no choice but to work for the landowners who had usurped their property. Because of the prejudice of their Protestant masters, many of them felt they had no alternative but to immigrate to America in search of a better life even before the potato famine. With next to nothing, they boarded overcrowded "coffin ships," which didn't have adequate food or water. As many as 250 passengers were expected to share thirty berths. Too many of the immigrating passengers never made it alive—strong men, delicate women and precious children alike. And many of these ships never made it across the ocean or capsized in sight of the shore when the unusually heavy-bottomed ships scraped underwater rocks they would have normally sailed over.

This cross-continental journey was a test of survival of the fittest, and the fittest were those who were most driven by pain, anger, fear, poverty and religious persecution.

Once in the United States, they quickly realized that arriving in America wasn't a magical key to happiness, and they also learned that the streets weren't paved with gold as they had believed. They arrived without resources, without capital to start businesses or buy farms and the prejudice they had experienced in Ireland was just as strong in America. "Irish need not apply…No Irish allowed inside," was plastered on doors of buildings and stores everywhere.

Fortunately, the greatest number of Irish immigrants arrived when America's economy was expanding at the advent of America's Industrial Revolution, and they were willing, ready and able to do the grunt work that was needed to mine the coal, build the canals and lay the rails for the national transportation system. Then they climbed onboard to be the first drivers, engineers and conductors.

They worked at unskilled and semiskilled jobs, even if they were talented craftsmen, but in doing so, they built the foundation for their children to become skilled plumbers, steamfitters, policemen and firefighters. As was their way, they worked hard and fought hard to attain and keep whatever they needed to survive, and for many at the end of the day, they found solace in a bottle of John Barleycorn—albeit a false sense of solace.

They soon found themselves in a position of losing it all when the "new immigrant" started to infiltrate the industries of which the Irish had just become part. Before long, they found themselves vying for positions against the new immigrant labor force from Italy, Poland and Hungary, leading to a vicious cycle of discrimination, polarization and brawls. Instead of welcoming the newcomers in a way that they themselves had not been welcomed, they were fearful and suspicious.

However, there is evidence that they put down their fists and helped one another in times of need. In W.W. Davis's *History of Bucks County*, he writes that during 1849, when the Asiatic cholera reared up again, it was brought to the Durham Furnace by a sick man on a canalboat. The lock tender, a man named Hough, was asked to look in on the boatman. He did, and then took sick a few days later and died. The disease spread throughout the village. In total, thirty people died; the epidemic took whole families or left young orphaned children. Despite the danger of being infected with this feared disease, women and men with Irish last names nursed each other.

> *The Irish immigrants, just arriving to work at the furnace, were the earliest victims. The wives of the workmen, a noble set of women, braved death in nursing the sick and preparing the dead for burial…and among the men, conspicuous for their services during this trying period, were Edward Keelon, John Young, Thomas and Farrel Riley, and Samuel F. Hartman. The widows and orphans of the cholera victims were cared for by the neighbors.*[60]

It didn't help that work on the canal was tedious. Some of the canallers picked fights to amuse themselves, or even pitted their mule-driving sons against the sons of other boatmen. All boatmen, even those who were normally even-tempered, could be aggressive when approaching a busy lock where they could be detained because of long queues.

> *Quarreling was often occasioned by one boatman stealing the locking turn of another, for instance while the crew of one boat slept another boat might pass by and take his place, after which a dispute and often a fight resulted.*[61]

For the most part, the Irish canal men weren't liked much in Bucks County, especially in the towns where they spent much of their time between trips, as in Bristol and Easton. In addition to boatmen, there were also about three hundred men who lived in Bristol and worked on the wharves there, screening, picking and transferring the coal to schooners. Their hard drinking and fisticuffs left the native residents feeling nothing more than contempt for them. Yet the fun-loving spirit of the Irish couldn't be ignored, either. They made up songs and funny little limericks, played musical instruments, wrote in journals and found ways to make the sometimes mind-numbing work go faster. Some Bucks Countians acknowledged their charms. *In War Times In Bristol*, Burnet Landreth writes:

> *Really in all their crudities they were a lovable class with their broad brogues, their laughable mistakes and fondness for fist fighting, but with a warm*

attachment for those in whom they had confidence. I recall some of these men whose joyous, sometimes laughable salutations it was a pleasure to return.[62]

Walking the Towpath

Boys who drove the mules along the canal towpath were either sons of boat captains or they hired out at the age of seven or eight to work as mule drivers. Some of them were redemptioners (indentured servants), sold right from the ship they arrived on. The day began before four o'clock in the morning and ended around midnight. They walked most of the way, anywhere from sixteen to twenty hours a day, usually barefoot, sometimes twenty-five miles. Their job was to currycomb, brush and harness the mules before dawn, hook up their traces to the boat, lead them throughout the long day, unharness them at around ten o'clock at night, allow the mules to roll and stretch, brush, feed and water them for the last time and stable them. Only then were the boys allowed to rest, and they slept for no more than four hours, usually fewer.

Children as young as six worked as mule drivers in the early years of the canal era. *Courtesy of the Pennsylvania Canal Society Collection, National Canal Museum, Easton, PA.*

In spite of their youth, they mastered difficult skills quickly. One of the most important lessons they learned right from the start was how to pass another boat coming in the opposite direction on the canal. If they didn't unhook their mules and drop the line properly when the other boat passed their boat, they risked their mules being pulled into the canal.

They were also responsible for snubbing the boat by wrapping the rope around a post to slow the boat's speed, and they had to do it right, for if the boat was going too fast, it could burn the rope through and enter the lock incorrectly, causing damage to either the boat or the lock, or both. Snubbing the boat was especially difficult when it was fully loaded and weighed as much as one hundred tons.

Learning how to be good canallers was the extent of their education. Except for the three midwinter months of December, January and February when the canal was not in operation, there was no time to attend school.

Although the boys were capable and had to grow up long before other boys their age, they were still just boys. The era was one that was filled with superstitions, especially for the immigrants, and there are accounts in several books that describe how frightening the walk could turn when the sun set and it was dark and quiet on the towpath. Sounds they could easily identify in the daylight sounded ominous in the dark, lonely countryside. That was when they appreciated the warm sides of their mules where they could nestle closer. Because of the long hours they worked, it wasn't uncommon for a mule driver to fall asleep on his feet and veer from the path into the canal. They often climbed up on the backs of their mules and fell sound asleep.

They dealt with snakes and eels crossing in front of them on the towpath, mosquito bites and bee stings. The sun beat down on them in the heat of summer, and there was no relief from pelting rain or snow in the cold months. They were warned not to walk too close to their mules during storms as the shoes attracted lightning. And for this work they earned five dollars a month.

The food was pretty good by all accounts, however. Breakfasts consisted of bacon or ham and eggs, bread and butter. The midday meal was cured meat, usually ham. A stew of meat with cabbage, potatoes and beans was a common dinner. Sometimes, when the canal men were lucky, they could abduct a stray chicken from a local farm, and they were notorious for "borrowing" corn in the late summer months from the rows that had been planted along the towpath. Honest boatmen, and they were in the majority, would leave a bag of coal as payment. Lock tenders sometimes sold fish that had just been taken from the Delaware or the canal, and because most of the lock tenders had large gardens or farmland near their houses, they would sell fresh vegetables to the canallers. Suppers were usually light—leftovers from dinner and possibly a piece of cake or pie brought from home.

On Sunday mornings, when there was very little movement on the canal since lock tenders didn't work on Sundays, the boatmen would enjoy mackerel or ham, fried potatoes and usually fresh-baked bread that they purchased from a lock tender's wife or at the local store. Sunday meals were always best and usually consisted of a roast of beef, with a pudding they called hunks-a-go pudding, which was essentially a typical Yorkshire pudding made with a batter of eggs, milk and flour poured into the grease and juices produced by the beef roast. They'd put a lid on the pan and let it cook on the stove until it was solid and steaming.

They worked hard, but they played hard, too, when they had the opportunity. The boys played marbles, dominoes, checkers and cat in the cradle with cord. They fished, played musical instruments and told tall tales to each other. Sometimes they boxed. Most of all, they enjoyed whatever much-needed rest and respite they could get on lazy Sunday afternoons.

The six-year-old mule drivers didn't know when they set off on foot along the towpath for the first time that it usually meant lifetime employment. They often became captains of their own boats, sometimes at as young as sixteen. The only qualification for captain was to be able to skillfully navigate a hinge boat through a lock.

Safeguarding the Canal

In addition to the tug captains who pulled the boats across the river from New Hope to Lambertville, the steamboat operators who pulled them from Bristol to the docks of Philadelphia and the superintendents hired by the LC&N to oversee the law along the canal and report to the canal commissioners regarding the conditions of the canal, the next most important canallers would be the maintenance crews.

They worked on dredgers, mud diggers, carpenter boats and flickers, and the work required long days, Monday through Saturday, and continued in the winter months. A crew of two men, called engineers, worked double shifts and shared the responsibilities of foreman on the mud diggers. One worked while the other slept and ate. They dredged the silt on the bottom of the canal to keep the depth required for boats to safely glide down the canal.

The carpenter boats were used to transport workers—sometimes as many as fifteen men—who would repair locks, bridges, company-owned houses and stables. Repairing a leak in the canal during operating months was complicated. The carpenters would build a "dam" around the spot, leaving enough room for a boat to pass, and pump the water out before using whatever materials would work to fill the crevice—rocks, straw, leaves—and then the area would be covered with clay. Once the clay hardened, the dam was removed and the water would cover the repaired area while they all kept their fingers crossed that the repair worked.

The men on the flicker boats kept the banks clean. They cut away weeds, bushes and tree branches that could choke the canal and hinder movement of the boats. The flicker operators also filled in holes along the towpath to prevent mules and drivers from breaking an ankle.

"Bank bosses" were responsible for their own sections of the canal, blacksmiths took care of shoes for the mules and repaired tools and objects made of metal used on the boats or at the locks and watchmen took care of the waste gates during heavy storms. All had their part to play, and all contributed to the success of the canal.

The cliffs at the Palisades in the "Narrows" rise abruptly along the river to three hundred feet, leaving very little room for the towpath and canal, but they contribute to the breathtaking scenery along the canal. *Courtesy of Historic Langhorne Association.*

When the Captains Were Kings

The boatmen made the transport of coal, iron ore, lumber and stone appear easy. But appearances aren't always what they seem, for each trip was at once backbreaking, dreary, dangerous and tedious. If the inventive geniuses of the newly formed nation were the brains of the American Industrial Revolution, it was the hardworking populace of America who were the backbone and muscle—the miners who dug out the coal, the carpenters who built and maintained the structures and boats, the firemen who worked the furnaces, the men who gripped the shovels to dig the channels and the laborers who laid the rails.

And during the rise of the "navigation revolution," it was the boat captains who were the kings of the narrow waterways. Their productive efforts during long, tiring days must be recognized as the valuable contribution it was to the economic growth of the country. Without the efficient and safe transportation of coal and other natural resources to the major cities of the East, the Industrial Revolution would have been much slower to evolve.

Each canalboat trip would begin when the boat captain pulled his boat up under the coal chutes at Mauch Chunk. Once his boat was loaded, he would move on to the weigh lock, get his paperwork from the lock tender there and then either continue on to Easton or wait until morning. Canaller Henry Darling said:

> *We'd tie up at one of the locks for the night. Then get an early start in the morning and be in Easton by 3 p.m., spend the night there, and be in Bristol by noon on the fourth day.*[63]

That was if everything went as expected along the way—no freshets (floods), no mishaps with the mules, no leaks in the canal, no problems at the locks, no holes in the boat.

They would begin their 106-mile trip that day, and when the canal season was over, if they were able to maintain a regular schedule, they would travel a distance of approximately 3,000 miles in that one season—normally lasting 212 days, sometimes more, sometimes less, depending on the weather.

Once in Bristol, if the tide was right, they would unhitch the mules, leave them stabled in Bristol and shove out into the Delaware River, where the tugs would pick them up and tow them to Philadelphia. If they worked for the company, they stayed in Bristol, were given another boat and started back up the canal, and if that was the case, the boatmen didn't always get a boat of equal quality to the one they had just surrendered. Sometimes the cabins would be infested with bedbugs; sometimes there was less room in the cabin or stoves didn't work as well as they had on the last boat.

Captain Pearl R. Nye, who had been born on a canalboat and was the fifteenth of eighteen children of an Erie Canalboat captain and his wife, spent much of his life collecting folk songs written about or by canal men. These songs, recorded between 1937 and 1938, are now located in the American Folklife Center at the Library of Congress. They uniquely describe and preserve the life of the nineteenth-century canal families. From one of those songs, "The Old Skipper," we get a glimpse of how they felt about their work.

There's tanbark and hoop poles, wet goods, merchandise,
Clay, coal, brick and lumber, cordwood, stone, and ice.
Yes, all that was needed, we boated, dear pal,
Best time of our lives we had on the canal.

I will not be a rover, for I love my boat,
I am happy, contented, yes work, dream and float.
My mules are not hungry, they're lively and gay,
The plank is pulled on, we are off on our way.[64]

Boatmen made anywhere from fourteen to twenty dollars a month, and some received around seventy-five cents to a dollar a ton for the coal they delivered. The company deducted 10 percent of their pay, and this money was given to them in January during the inactive winter. They always tried to make the return trip from Bristol to Easton profitable by carrying merchandise that arrived in Bristol's port for the local residents along the canal. If they were private captains, they paid tolls at several locks along the Delaware Canal. If they worked for the company, their boat number was logged and sent to the company.

A crew of three was required at the beginning of the canal age. In *The Whig* newspaper, on June 15, 1836, Supervisor Joseph Hough published this notice:

To boatmen on the Delaware Canal
It will hereafter be required for every boat navigating on the Delaware
Division Pennsylvania Canal, to have a Steersman and Bowsman on
each boat, either descending or ascending said Canal, and also a boy
with the tow horse.

That rule didn't last long once the company ascertained that a crew of two could handle operation of the boat. Having a smaller crew, however, left them more vulnerable to problems that would arise.

Traveling in an open boat along a readily accessible route, with a towpath on one side and a berm on the other and surrounded by deserted farmland for most of the trip, boatmen could be victimized by bandits. There was a canalboat captain named John Reigal who carried a pouch of gold pieces around with him to settle his debts and pay for his provisions. His fellow canal men told him how dangerous this was, but it took quite a while before he was convinced that putting his gold in a bank was safer. Reports of theft along the canal finally persuaded him.

It wasn't uncommon for people to "rob" coal from the hold when a captain left his boat for some reason, and that would reflect on him when the coal was delivered and weighed. Even some lock tenders would "raid" a boat and sell the extra coal to make some money.

In truth, many boatmen themselves benefited from selling coal along the route, and it was gravely frowned upon by the company, which hired a Pinkerton agent to investigate. The LC&N expected some of the coal on a boat to "disappear" and considered it a hazard of the business. It wasn't always deliberate on the part of the boatmen; the "shovellers" who took the coal off the boat at the destinations along the way weren't always very careful, and coal, called "sweepings," accumulated at the bottom of the hold. Other times, the shovellers were careless on purpose, especially when a bottle of Bushkill whiskey was involved. In 1890, the company hired the Pinkerton Detective Agency to find out who of the boatmen were the worst offenders, and they sent an undercover agent to hitch rides on the boats to observe. Although most of the boat captains were careful not to talk too much, the agent was able to report some captains. He even reported that at one of the hotels along the canal, the "hookers" would go onboard and carry off some of the coal for use in the hotel while the boatman went inside for a quick beer.[65] In the last years of the canal age, a seal was put on the hatches after the coal was loaded, and it didn't bode well for the boatmen if the seal was broken when they delivered their load.

The camelback bridges that crossed over the canal may be picturesque, but they were nuisances for the canal men. When a boat was light and riding higher on the water, clearance under the bridges was too low, and many boatmen were injured. Ill-behaved children and teenagers were known to throw rocks or food over the bridges at the canal men, then run away laughing. In some of the rougher areas along the route, there were incidences when containers of trash were thrown on the canalboats. In one episode, a canal man was cooking his breakfast on deck when one of the

The camelback bridges along the canal are picturesque, but boatmen considered them a hazard. There wasn't much headroom beneath the bridges, and people standing on them would sometimes throw rocks or garbage at the boats. *Courtesy of Historic Langhorne Association.*

boys urinated down into the pan. The canallers' irritation was compounded by the fact that it was difficult for a canal man to jump off the boat in time to catch the miscreants.

And then there were the swimmers who thought nothing of grabbing onto the boat for a ride, which could create a delay or even damages to either the boat or the sides of the canal if the captain couldn't steer properly. Some captains were good-natured about it, and often the swimmers would acquiesce quickly and allow the boat to move on, but sometimes not. One captain reported in Yoder's *Delaware Canal Journal*, "So there were these two in a canoe who grabbed on my rudder. I said, 'Please get off it's hard for me to steer.'" When the two wouldn't comply, the captain went down into the cabin, grabbed his chamber pot and threw the entire contents onto the culprits. "You ought to see them dive for water. They took the boat number and from that time on we had no more trouble."[66] Some captains realized that they would avoid more trouble if they were agreeable. Captain Joe Reed would let them get on and dive off, and before long the boys could be coaxed to let him move on.

Although there were 116 regulations devised by the canal commissioners at the beginning of canal operations in 1833, there were really only a few important rules that couldn't be violated. The passing rule was one of them. The loaded boats stayed toward the berm side, and the lighter empty boats

Several covered bridges, like this one in Uhlersville, crossed over the canal and continue to be part of the Bucks County landscape today. *Courtesy of Historic Langhorne Association.*

moved along the towpath side, having the right of way. The towline of the loaded boat was dropped to the bottom of the canal so the approaching boat could pass over it. Every boat had to have a guard plate attached to the keel, extending under the rudder to cover the opening between the sternpost and rudder to prevent fouling the towline. If a boat was found without that guard, the captain would be penalized with a fine and have to pay for all damages.

When boats passed going in the same direction, the slow boat was expected to move to the berm side, stop and allow the other boat to pass. Again, a twenty-dollar penalty was charged if this regulation was violated. But a violation of this sort would often lead to a fight long before the canal bosses even knew about it, and in one incident of record, the violence turned to murder.

Captain Thomas Dougherty stopped his boat, but it wasn't tied up, and the bow drifted out into the canal and blocked the passing of a boat operated by John Wildonger. Wildonger asked Dougherty to move the boat several times, but Dougherty did nothing. As a result, an argument ensued, with Wildonger throwing a watermelon rind at Dougherty and Dougherty responding by throwing chunks of coal. Wildonger threw his ice hook at Dougherty, striking him in the neck. The injured man fell overboard and was pulled out by the captain of a third boat, Captain James Thompson. Dougherty died a few minutes later. At his trial, Wildonger and his crew testified that he acted in self-defense, although Thompson contradicted that story. After an hour of deliberation, the jury inexplicably returned a verdict of not guilty.

When the hinge boats were empty, the middle portion of the vessel was slightly lower than the bow and stern, and in order to compensate, the canal captains attached turnbuckles to cleats on each half at the hinge that would draw the center of the boat up to allow for easier towing and steering, especially along areas of the canal that were more difficult to navigate. One of those points was a six-mile stretch just above Ground Hog lock.

At this section of the canal, a team of mules pulling a loaded boat stopped for a drink at the overflow. The driver happened to be on the boat at the time with the captain. Because of the strong current, the boat didn't slow up and it passed the mules. Before the men onboard could react, the mules were drawn into the canal and were pulled down by their harnesses and traces. A Newfoundland dog that was on the boat jumped into the canal, grabbed the lead mule's bridle and pulled the mules to shore.[67]

Stone walls along the canal in New Hope were built with spikes to keep the canallers off the walls while they waited for their turn to go through the locks. *Author's collection.*

The wiser farmers and residents along the canal took advantage of the monotony of the trip up and down the canal for the boatmen. If the boatmen were accused of helping themselves to a wayward chicken crossing the towpath and dining on fat, ripe tomatoes that had been growing along the berm, then it was fair game when farmers placed bottles along their fences, knowing that the bored boatmen would be unable to resist the temptation to pitch coal to see how many bottles they could knock down. In a good year, the farmers could warm their homes for many days and nights with the coal they collected after one of these challenges.

Where There Are Kings, There Are Queens

The wives and children of boatmen either lived on the boat year-round with the captains or took several trips with them during the summer months. Wives could be as durable and capable as their husbands. They cooked, they steered and, when necessary, they drove the mules and snubbed the boat at the locks.

One day Dr. Magill of New Hope, a man who was very respected by the canallers, was fetched to deliver a baby on one of the canalboats. The physician made it just in time to deliver the baby, then left mother and child on the cabin's bunk to go on his rounds. He was astounded to find the new mother at the tiller of the boat the very next morning, her infant in the other arm.

The women gave birth to their babies on the boats, tied their children to the decks of the boats so that they wouldn't fall off and did their best to make the tiny cabins homey and warm. They bathed themselves and their children in the cold water of the canal, and come wash day, the women would bring their wooden washtubs on deck to launder their clothes and hang a line from one end of the boat to the other to dry them. The "facilities" were the bushes along the towpath or a pail or chamber pot in the cabin. Even in the best of circumstances, a boat provided primitive accommodations.

In good weather, and especially when wives would take the trip with their husbands, tie-up areas were filled with music and dancing. Accordions, violins and harmonicas came out of the cabins, and everyone was in good voice, singing songs about canal life, with new lyrics written and put to the melodies of songs from the "old country." The Germans yodeled, the Irish waxed poetic and *all* danced to waltzes and polkas. They put aside their disagreements and fatigue and celebrated life as only hardworking, life-loving folk can do.

During the Civil War, when the canal men went off to fight, many of their wives, daughters and sons too young to fight took over the

Boatmen often brought their families with them for occasional trips, and sometimes families lived on the canal year-round. *Courtesy of the Pennsylvania Canal Society Collection, National Canal Museum, Easton, PA.*

operations of the boats and locks. Although it was a hard life for women, supporting their children while their husbands fought a war was impetus enough to leave their homes on land for the cabins of their snappers and hinge boats.

The Turnout

When the canal needed to be repaired for major damages, usually as a result of freshets or storms, the canal men didn't work, and there was no such thing as unemployment insurance then. When the "season" was cut short, so were the wages. Damages from the flood of 1841 were still being made in 1843, and the boatmen who had anticipated a prosperous year were bitterly disappointed when a series of additional breaks in the banks occurred just as they started down the canal.

Boats were backed up in Easton. Canallers sat on their coal-filled boats with nowhere to go and nothing to do, their tempers growing hotter as they realized that the delays would result in lower wages for yet another year. They gathered in groups, railing against the company and becoming more inflamed as another sixty days went by without work.

When the canal was finally opened, the boatmen declared a "turnout," meaning they were on strike. They demanded assurance of regular work and higher wages to make up for the pay they had lost. The Mauch Chunk miners joined them in solidarity, much to the dismay of Josiah White and the LC&N. They held their ground as long as they could, but in the end, the boatmen lost. And when they went back to work after their strike, they had gained nothing, but had lost even more time and more wages.

Chapter 9

Human Cargo

They came in the dark of night. They huddled in secret subterranean rooms. They crawled through underground tunnels. They buried themselves in straw-filled wagons. And they stowed away inside the coal holds of canalboats.

The North Star was their guide. They were always looking north, running north, racing toward their right to be free and to be treated with equality.

During the early years of settlement, Pennsylvanians, including Quakers, owned slaves. The doctrines of the Quaker religion were contrary to the practice of slavery and very strong Quaker opponents began to rail against their brethren who seemed to disregard the precepts that all people were equal in the sight of God. Even George Fox, who was the founder of the Society of Friends, preached against slavery but didn't take strong action against it. William Penn was himself a slave owner, with several slaves serving at Pennsbury Manor, his country home in Bucks County.

But those who believed slavery was immoral began to travel throughout Quaker towns and villages, preaching that it was an aberration to the Quaker faith. One of these men was Anthony Benezet, a French-born Quaker who was renowned for his fight against slavery. He was able to convince Benjamin Franklin and Benjamin Rush to lead the Pennsylvania Society for Promoting the Abolition of Slavery. Soon, other prominent abolitionists—such as Lucretia Mott, Anna Dickinson, Ann Preston, Jane Swisshelm and Susan B. Anthony—became more vocal in supporting the cause against slavery. The Pennsylvania Abolition Society raised funds to purchase slaves and immediately set them free. Thaddeus Stevens, who was elected to the House of Representatives in 1859, was an unrelenting foe of slavery.

In March 1780, the Act for the Gradual Abolition of Slavery was passed by the Pennsylvania Assembly. It called for the *gradual* release of every Negro and mulatto child born within the state after the act was passed. Once

The gristmill in Yardley, which is located along the canal, was also a "station" on the underground railroad. *Author's collection.*

released, they would be given the same rights as servants that had been bound by indenture for four years. It wasn't perfect, but it was a start, and slavery did decline in Pennsylvania after the passing of this act.

There was a large settlement of former slaves located in Columbia, Pennsylvania. This settlement was a refuge for those who fled from bondage in Virginia, Maryland and other Southern regions close to Pennsylvania. Once the fleeing slaves reached that area, slaveholders had a very difficult time finding them. Before long, the slaveholders were saying that slaves must be escaping in some sort of "underground railroad." The expression took hold, and soon there were "conductors" who guided "passengers" from "station" to "station" (homes or buildings that would hide them). Then there were "stockholders," who financed the organization. Secrecy was crucial to success, and as a result there are very few documents that lay out the routes, name the slaves or identify the "railroad workers."

Many of the stationmasters and conductors were free black men, but without the assistance of the Pennsylvania, New York and New Jersey white abolitionists and sympathizers to the cause of freedom, they could not have been as successful as they were. Mostly Quakers, they housed, fed and

Underground railroad researcher Millard Mitchell stands in front of the historic library in Yardley. *Author's collection.*

clothed the fugitive slaves, then passed them on to the next conductor. They learned the code words and symbols, and they worked in the middle of the night. They knew very little about the next station or the people involved so that when the slave catchers came to their doors, they really wouldn't have much to tell. They were breaking the law, and they risked the freedom of their own African American friends and servants. Under the Fugitive Slave Law of 1850, suspected fugitives had no right to a jury trial and could not testify on their own behalf when brought before a magistrate. Free black men and women could be taken by slave hunters and forced into slavery if they were "suspected" of being fugitive slaves. As a result, Pennsylvanians were silent about their work and brought as little attention to themselves and the work they were doing as possible.

The main line of the escape path through Pennsylvania was primarily by way of York, Adams, Lancaster and Chester Counties. Bucks County was the "Fourth Road" in the escape route of fugitive slaves from the South, and it ran from 1840 to 1850. The Bucks County route was less used, yet many slaves came through the county and went on to reach Canada.

During speaking engagements and when talking to students, Millard Mitchell uses photographs, maps and newspaper articles to tell the story of the fleeing slaves who made their way through Bucks County during the years of the underground railroad. *Author's collection.*

The fugitives traveled in constant fear all night long and rested in hiding places during the day. They believed that discovery was just around the next bend, at the next barn or in the next cellar. The route in Bucks zigzagged to elude pursuit, but most accounts recall that it started in Bristol, moved through Morrisville, Yardley, Langhorne, Newtown, Wrightstown, Buckingham, New Hope and almost always ended in Quakertown at the home of Richard Moore, the last stop of the underground railroad in Bucks County. There are accounts of numerous tunnels throughout the county that connect one station to another.

Stories, given to us from recollections by reliable sources in Bucks County, also point out places along the river and canal that were stations, and it makes sense that the Delaware Canal was a route on the underground railroad, just as the Delaware and Hudson, Erie, Morris and Ohio Canals all claim to have been.

Millard C. Mitchell, the foremost authority on the underground railroad in Bucks County (particularly in Yardley), reports "I've seen very little in writing due to the fact that the underground railroad was secret—everything was secretly done for protection from prosecution from the Fugitive Slave Law." Yet, Mr. Mitchell has met and interviewed several residents of Yardley and other towns along the canal who have verified stories handed down from generations of canallers. When Mitchell, who is originally from North Carolina and is the grandson of a fugitive slave, first moved to Yardley in 1956, he found that several of his neighbors and new friends were the grandsons of operators in the underground railroad. He also visited the subterranean rooms in several of the buildings and homes in Yardley that hid men, women and children on their flight to freedom. Upon receiving information from what he discerned to be "very reliable sources," he visited cemeteries and looked at records to authenticate that those people who were assumed to be participants in the underground railroad were alive during the years before the Civil War and worked in occupations that would attest to their availability to help. According to Mitchell:

There was an African American minister of the AME Methodist Church in Yardley, a Rev. Miller, who was instrumental in securing places in Yardley to hide the fugitive slaves. There were about ten stations in Yardley.

The Continental Tavern was one of the "stations" on the underground railroad. Tunnels from the canal connected several buildings and homes in Yardley where runaway slaves could hide. *Courtesy of the Continental Hotel.*

Four stations were very close to the canal: the town's general store, the Continental Tavern (which was a temperance house at the time), the gristmill and Lakeside, a private home facing Lake Afton that backs up to the canal.

The Continental Tavern has recently been renovated by new owner Frank Lyons, who was proud to share information about a stone-walled, dirt-floor chamber in the lowest level of the building that can be entered at this time through a trapdoor only. Other parts of the cellar of the building are readily accessible and show evidence of a shop and other common uses, but there is no way into this secret chamber from any other part of the building.

Additionally, there is a well-shaped hole in the hidden chamber that could have been used to allow the entry of fugitives from an underground tunnel that is reported to come directly from the canal bank. As layers of the dirt floor are excavated, Lyons and his workers are finding artifacts from each era—there is very strong evidence that the Continental was a speakeasy during Prohibition, as they found ten to fifteen thousand bottles, whole and broken in every size and shape, from that era. As they dig deeper into the floor of the chamber, they hope to find further evidence of the underground

This trapdoor leads to a chamber in the lower level of the Continental Hotel. Although there is access to other parts of the basement in this building, the only entrance to this chamber is by the trapdoor in the kitchen of the tavern. *Courtesy of the Continental Hotel.*

railroad. With Millard Mitchell's assistance, Lyons intends to rebuild the chamber and add the kind of furniture and utensils that would have been there before the Civil War for patrons to view.

Mitchell has seen similar subterranean chambers in other homes and buildings in Yardley that had been kept intact, a whisper that confirms the courage of people who wanted to do right and the determination of refugees who fled tyranny and slavery to seek freedom.

Fugitive slaves would travel up from the lower portion of Pennsylvania through Germantown, which was occupied mainly by German Quakers who were strong abolitionists, and in the cover of night they would go to the docks in Philadelphia where the coal boats had just been emptied of their cargoes. The boatmen—African American, Quaker and even Irish and German sympathizers—would usher their human cargo into the holds and close the hatches, undoubtedly with provisions of food and water.

From Philadelphia, the boats would be pulled by steamboat back to the Bristol basin and into the Delaware Division Canal, where the boatmen would begin the return trip to Mauch Chunk. According to Mitchell, there was a lookout point on River Road just south of Yardley, where a sympathizer watched from the top of his house to see if the militia from

This is a chamber that is believed to have been a hiding place of runaway slaves. *Courtesy of the Continental Hotel.*

Frank Lyons, owner of the Continental Tavern, is excavating the secret chamber and cistern that is located in the basement of the restaurant to find the tunnel that is alleged to connect to the canal. *Courtesy of the Continental Hotel.*

the barracks in Trenton was on the way across the bridge in search of lawbreakers. If he saw activity, he'd send an alarm out to the boats and other stationmasters and conductors.

It was a one-day trip from Bristol to Yardley, where the boats would tie up, the mules would be stabled and the fugitives would be guided to a hideout in one of the stations closest to the canal. They would be fed and have a chance to rest. Depending upon the "climate" in the region, the fugitives would either return to the boat before dawn to continue their escape to the north, or they would be hidden in a wagon and taken in another direction, probably through Attleborough (now Langhorne), just a few short miles from Yardley, which also was a safe haven for fugitive slaves. Sometimes the slaves would stay in Yardley for a few weeks, working in the gristmill or on local Quaker farms to earn some money before they moved on to the next station.

Sadly, many of the conductors and stationmasters never found out what happened to the hopeful people they helped. Few letters were sent since the majority of slaves hadn't been educated and didn't know how to write, and even if a newspaper article was published along the route relating the

Right: During excavation of the chamber, this canalboat "night hawker" was found in the rubbish. *Courtesy of the Continental Hotel.*

Below: Houses like this one located on the Delaware River are reported to have been used as lookout locations to watch for slave hunters or militia crossing from New Jersey. If seen, an alert would be sent into town to move or hide the fugitive slaves. *Author's collection.*

A row of quaint houses on Canal Street in Yardley overlooks the now peaceful waterway. *Author's collection.*

capture of a fugitive slave, it normally didn't make it to other municipalities. The "operatives" didn't know if those they helped were captured or living free in Canada. They had only their own consciences to tell them that the guarded work they had done was righteous and compassionate.

Chapter 10

The Canal's Worst Enemy

From Freshets to Floods

The Delaware Division Canal and the Lehigh Navigation Canal endured both freshets and floods, and did so frequently. Melting snow and ice coming from the hills and mountains surrounding the canal caused the streams and creeks to overflow several times a year. Although both the Delaware and Lehigh Canals were built to cope with these freshets, there were years that spring rains and raging storms created greater flooding than the canals were designed to handle, causing breaches and damaged banks.

The Delaware River floods were not as frequent as the freshets, but when the river did flood, it was usually catastrophic for the river towns. One of the major flaws of the Delaware Division Canal was the fact that it was built so close to the river.

The first freshet to damage the canal was in March 1832, not long after it had opened. In January 1839, a violent storm descended on New York, New Jersey, Delaware and Pennsylvania, causing flooding across those states and major damages to the canals, except for the Lehigh Navigation Canal, which suffered very little from the storm.

The Delaware Canal suffered major breeches when the flood reached twenty-two feet above the low-water mark. It flooded all the lower levels of the canal, swept off aqueducts and filled the canal with soil from the destroyed banks.

The dam at Easton was almost completely destroyed, but the local residents and canal workers moved as one force to rebuild it, even during a raging current in the cold month of January. But the cost of repairing the canal that month was overwhelming.

The flood of 1841, caused by heavy rains melting the snow in the mountains, nearly destroyed both the Delaware Division and Lehigh Navigation Canals. It carried away locks, dams, houses, boats and bridges.

Floods from the Delaware River frequently put the canal out of commission for weeks, months and even years. This photo was taken near the River House (Chez Odette's) and shows the canal completely underwater. *Courtesy of the New Hope Historical Society.*

This January flood was especially devastating to the Lehigh Navigation Canal, which had escaped major damage in 1839. The winter flood was followed by more that same year, in June, July and August, and as quickly as the damage was repaired, there was more damage to be fixed.

The LC&N called Josiah White out of semiretirement and employed an engineer, E.A. Douglas, to determine the entire damage. It took months to repair both waterways, and that year toll collection dropped to $64,974.93 as the expenses rose to $109,338.81.[68] The floods of 1841 nearly bankrupted the LC&N.

Faults in the construction of the Delaware Division—shortcuts taken during its construction—contributed to the damages. After the floods of 1841, guard gates were incorporated into the design of the canal, and they did seem to relieve damage from flooding to some extent. However, the region was still plagued by floods: in the spring of 1843, in the fall of 1845 and again in 1850, 1852, 1862 and 1868. All of this flooding interrupted boating from a month to several months. During some of these floods, families lost their homes, businessmen lost their businesses and, sadly, some lost their lives. When the waters subsided, logs, boats, houses, bridges and dead livestock littered the river towns along the Delaware. The early twentieth century wasn't kinder with high waters, floods and freshets in 1901, 1902, 1904 and 1906.

This photo shows the Yardley Inn underwater during one of the many floods that plague Bucks County towns and boroughs even to this day. *Courtesy of the Yardley Inn.*

In March 1936, when the transfer of the Delaware Canal to the state was being discussed, a statewide storm produced disastrous floods in all of the river valleys. And repairs were necessary once again when Hurricane Diane swept through eastern Pennsylvania and caused yet another flood that took a heavy toll in the form of human life and property.

In fact, the Delaware Valley is vulnerable to this day, with heavy flooding from the Delaware River, brought on primarily by overflows from two New York reservoirs and a mountain lake in Pennsylvania.

Chapter 11

Beautiful Impressions

The Delaware Division Canal passes through some of the most picturesque landscapes in the United States. In some places it is breathtaking. The canal meanders through beautiful countryside, sandwiched between the Delaware Canal on one side and neatly laid-out farms, charming little colonial villages and wildflower-laden fields on the other.

Its beauty was not lost on some of the most renowned American impressionists of the nineteenth and twentieth centuries. Members of what are called Pennsylvania impressionists and the New Hope School, these artists came from many parts of the country to Pennsylvania to study and teach at the Pennsylvania Academy of Fine Arts in Philadelphia. The circle was formed in 1898, when many of them made their homes in the tiny hamlets and villages along the Delaware Canal and established their studios in and around New Hope.

A noted painter and critic of the time, Guy Pène du Bois, declared that their work was "our first truly national expression." It is impossible to say which of them is the most famous, for all have made their marks in American collectors' hearts. They reflect life as it was in small-town America during the late 1800s and the early 1900s, and they portray the beauty of the landscape before paved roadways and unsightly telephone and electric poles and wires blemished the views of magnificent barns, beautiful rivers and Victorian villages.

The New Hope Artists

Edward W. Redfield may have won the most awards of any American artist except John Singer Sargent. Redfield would tie his canvasses to trees in the brutal winter weather in order to paint a perfect winter scene, yet his spring and summer paintings are just as moving and his city skyline paintings are

The New Hope Circle of American impressionists was fascinated by the Delaware Canal and often used it as a model for its paintings and sketches. This is John Fulton Folinsbee's *Mule Barn*. *Courtesy of Gratz Gallery, New Hope, PA.*

renowned. After studying in Philadelphia, France, Italy and England, he settled in Centre Bridge in 1898. He was one of the first American artists to paint on location and complete a painting in one session.

William Langson Lathrop was instrumental in establishing this special community of artists when he moved to Phillips Mill in 1899. He brought his students to his studio, and his wife, Anne, hosted weekly teas for his colleagues. He never took formal training, but instead learned from many artists he admired, and, in turn, he mentored several members of the New Hope School's first and second generation of artists. He was beloved and greatly missed when his boat sank in Long Island during a hurricane in 1938 and he drowned.

Daniel Garber, who lived in Lumberville, was born in Indiana and settled on the Cuttalossa Creek. He taught at the Pennsylvania Academy of the Fine Arts, and his work won numerous national awards.

After visiting Lathrop's New Hope home, Florence and Henry Snell, both acclaimed artists from England, relocated to the village. Florence won the

Fern Coppedge, *Canal in Winter. Courtesy of Gratz Gallery, New Hope, PA.*

McMillan landscape prize from the Association of Women Painters and Sculptors in New York in 1913. Henry taught at the Philadelphia School of Design for Women from 1899 to 1943.

Fern Isabel Coppedge may be the artist who painted the largest number of Bucks County landscapes, although some of her art was produced in Gloucester, Massachusetts, when she spent summers there. Like Redfield, she tied her canvasses to trees during winter storms, and she was fastidious in her attention to the effects of changing light on a landscape. She became a member of the "Philadelphia Ten," a group of women painters who banded together to show their work in exhibitions once a year. In April 1922, the *Christian Science Monitor* published this statement about this group of American artists:

> *While a certain coterie of men artists are striving for "atmosphere" and find in harshness of subject and technique what purports to be the strength and power of masculine intelligence, the traditions of the decorative and beautiful are being perpetuated quietly, conscientiously, by the sisters of the brush.*[69]

John Fulton Folinsbee, *Lock, New Hope. Courtesy of Gratz Gallery, New Hope, PA.*

It is easy to understand why artists and early photographers were so attracted to the Delaware Division Canal. *Courtesy of Historic Langhorne Association.*

Most of these artists lived beyond the end of the canal age, long after the Delaware Canal had ceased to be an avenue of commerce. They witnessed the once busy canal become empty, one boat after another disappearing from the water, its rough and ready captains and the young mule drivers in bare feet passing their studios less and less frequently. The sound of the tinkling bells and padded hoofbeats of the mules faded. Yet most of the artists remained living and working on the now quiet and peaceful canal—perhaps they liked it even better in its serenity.

Artists are still drawn to the canal's beauty. In a 2007 summer boat excursion on the Delaware Canal with the New Hope Canal Boat Company, two artists were seen sitting—one on the towpath and one on the berm—their canvasses in front of them, their paint-stained palettes beside them, as they immortalized the present canal just as Redfield, Schofield, Lathrop, Coppedge, Folinsbee and Wagner had during the previous century.

Chapter 12

National Historic Landmark

The seminal role of the canals in the ferment of the Industrial Revolution is little appreciated today. Yet it can be traced directly to Josiah White and Erskine Hazard, owners of the Lehigh Coal and Navigation Company, and their quest for expanding markets for their coal…The decline of the canals started with the building of the railroads and continued with the adoption of coke as the primary fuel for smelting iron. As more rail lines were built…less traffic went by the canal.

—*Ann Bartholomew and Lance Metz,* Delaware and Lehigh Canals

Demise of the Canals

During the years that the Pennsylvania canals enjoyed moderate success as a major transportation mode for moving coal, lumber and other goods, the railroads were being established as well. New immigrants arriving in America were being put to work laying the rails in all directions, while better and bigger steam engines were built.

After the Civil War, the country experienced a wave of prosperity, followed by a severe economic panic in 1873 that affected the entire nation. As a result of government-promoted speculative credit, there was a huge overexpansion of the nation's railroad network. The Coinage Act of 1873 created a depreciation of silver. A chain of bank failures caused the stock market to close for ten days. Numerous railroads went bankrupt, and businesses failed. It was also the beginning of the decline of the Lehigh Coal and Navigation Company.

In 1866, at the height of the canal era, 792,000 tons of coal were pulled upon the canal annually. In 1915, that amount dropped to 130,000 tons, and in 1931, only 65,000 tons moved from Easton to Bristol.[70] With the arrival of the freight trains, the American canals began to decline.

Railroads took over as the most efficient means of transporting anthracite coal and other cargo in the mid- to late nineteenth century, and the once busy canals became obsolete. *Courtesy of the Historic Langhorne Association.*

Additionally, roadways were being improved, and the automobile was taking over as the most expedient and popular means of transportation, followed by the sturdier truck. Use of canals in other parts of the country was decreasing rapidly in the late part of the nineteenth century. Coal was still the predominant fuel for homes and industry in the early part of the twentieth century, but now the coal companies were using rail and automotive means to transport it to even the smallest towns and villages, and trucks brought the coal right up to the houses, mills and factories.

The only reason the Delaware Canal lasted as long as it did was due to the fact that Delaware Canal coal yards still needed deliveries, and unlike most of the other canals in the country that stopped operations in the late 1800s, there was no parallel railroad from Easton to Bristol along the Delaware Division. It wasn't until the autumn of 1931 that the Lehigh Coal and Navigation Company ended all commercial navigation on the canal when the costs of the operation couldn't be supported by the diminishing revenue.

Delaware State Park and Landmark Designation

The canal was left to the leisure boaters and Sunday picnics that had always been popular along the picturesque and now peaceful Delaware Canal. Nature took over as the company's nurturing of the canal declined, and it fell into disrepair, especially after floods and freshets. Residents along the canal who believed in the importance of its history and who loved its beauty worried that it would be lost forever and that the LC&N would give it to the state to pave over and make into a roadway. Committed individuals formed a group called the Delaware Valley Protective Association and lobbied the LC&N to deed the land and the canal to the commonwealth as a gift to the people of Pennsylvania. They succeeded, and on the very same day that the last empty canalboat made its return trip from Bristol to Easton, the LC&N deeded forty miles of the canal to Pennsylvania.

The ceremonial transfer took place on October 18, 1931, on the grounds of the Thompson-Neely Mill, a segment of Washington Crossing Historic Park. Governor Gifford Pinchot accepted the deed from William Jay Turner, general counsel for the LC&N. Numerous dignitaries attended, joined by preservation, historical, nature and artistic groups. In his speech,

Ceremonies marking the transfer of most of the Delaware Division Canal lands from the Lehigh Coal and Navigation Company to the State of Pennsylvania took place on the historic Thompson-Neeley farm, which is now part of the Washington Crossing Historic Park. *Author's collection.*

The canal runs through the Thompson-Neely farm and past the cemetery, where soldiers of the Continental army were buried in unmarked graves during the Revolutionary War. *Author's collection.*

Governor Pinchot declared that all the bridges that crossed the canal would be preserved to "continue to help make the historic canal one of the beauty spots in the United States."[71]

He named the stretch of park the Roosevelt State Park in honor of fellow preservationist and close friend Teddy Roosevelt. To confirm this sentiment on the part of the LC&N, William Turner said that the company had deeded the canal, the towpath and the berm along the canal "to assure perpetuity of the beautiful landscape we have all enjoyed these many years."[72] The LC&N would remain in control of the canals above Easton and would in fact continue to provide the water for the Delaware Division from the slack water of the Lehigh River at Easton.

There were very interesting plans surrounding the formation of the park. The plans called for three major centers in the park, four minor centers and five special centers, and all would provide canoe and boat concessions. There would be dance boats, repair boats and cabin boats so that families could spend vacations on the canal. Jobs would be created with these concessions, and the state would hire supervisors, foremen, laborers, carpenters and other employees to staff facilities and operate the locks.

None of these wonderful plans came to fruition. Once again, floods and freshets took their toll and the park had all it could do to keep the canal from falling in upon itself.

By 1936, no one wanted to take responsibility for the canal's repairs. James F. Bogardus, who was the deputy secretary of forests and waters, announced that the granting of a portion of the canal was unconstitutional. He claimed that this explained why the state wasn't responsible for repairing the aqueduct at Point Pleasant that had been badly damaged by a flood—the LC&N still owned it and was responsible for its repair. The LC&N refused to assume responsibility, although the company did make minor repairs. The arguments and litigation went on until 1940, while residents along the canal where the water was stagnant complained of mosquitoes, unsightly weeds and general dismay about what was supposed to be an active waterway.

In 1947, the state finally appropriated $200,000 toward work on the canal, starting with the Point Pleasant aqueduct. Water would fill the canal again. However, the Durham aqueduct collapsed. It was repaired by 1951, but in 1955 the entire Delaware Valley was devastated by floods brought

The Delaware Canal as it is today in front of Chez Odette's, both of which suffered major damage during recent floods. *Author's collection.*

on by Hurricane Diane, and repairs on the canal would cost as much as $300,000.

The canal was never to be completely filled with water again. Standing water that was present in sections wasn't suitable for swimming, and in many places the water wasn't high enough for boating of any sort. There were additional hazards such as fallen trees, cave-ins and litter—picnic tables, chairs, pieces of cars, shopping carts. A small section of the canal was covered over with a parking lot.

Yet efforts on behalf of the beautiful historic waterway never ended. In 1974, in response to an application prepared by C.P. Yoder, then the curator of the National Canal Museum in Easton, the canal was placed on the National Register of Historic Places. Due to further efforts made by Bucks County residents like Virginia Forrest and the Swope brothers, who had been canallers since childhood, the canal was dedicated a National Historic Landmark and the towpath a National Recreation Trail in 1978. The length of the canal was renamed the Delaware Canal State Park.

In 1989, the Delaware and Lehigh Navigation Canal National Heritage Corridor was created by Congress, which allows the National Park Service to assist state and local governments and private agencies to preserve and interpret the canal. The corridor's mission is to preserve heritage and conserve green space for public use in Bucks, Carbon, Lehigh, Luzerne and Northampton Counties in Pennsylvania.

Best Friends

Never doubt that a small group of thoughtful, committed citizens can change the world; indeed it is the only thing that ever has.
—*Margaret Mead*

The canal's many enthusiasts began to gather together in 1982 under the leadership of Betty Orlemann and called their nonprofit organization Friends of the Delaware Canal (FODC). Their vision is to restore and improve the canal, towpath and berm. It is their greatest desire to restore the water continuously from Easton to Bristol.

Orlemann recruited friends, neighbors and legislators to help with the preservation of the beloved canal. They piled into boats and pulled on high boots to clean out the debris and weeds. Jim Greenwood, who was a Pennsylvania state senator at the time, became a member of the Friends of the Delaware Canal and secured $50,000 from the Pennsylvania Department of Commerce to create a master plan for the repair and improvement of the

The lock tender's house at Lock 11 in New Hope was completely restored and is now the headquarters of the Friends of the Delaware Canal (FODC). *Author's collection.*

canal. With input from the communities along the canal, FODC and other canal authorities, a consultant developed a plan that called for $32 million worth of work. In the meantime, with money they raised on canal walks, lectures and parties, the FODC repainted some of the camelback bridges over the canal, and organized school and service organizations in cleanup projects.

According to Susan Taylor, executive director of FODC:

> *This master plan created a vision that was able to be implemented. Many of the ideas and projects outlined in the plan have been completed, and we've received a great deal of support from the Pennsylvania Department of Conservation and Natural Resources.*

After receiving donations from individuals and businesses and grants from the Delaware and Lehigh National Heritage Corridor and the Pew Charitable Trusts, the FODC restored the lock tender's house at Lock 11 in New Hope and established its headquarters and interpretation center there. The FODC inspired the creation of a state legislative caucus in

Mick Drustrup, Ginger Budny and Betty Orlemann of the FODC paint one of the camelback bridges. The organization works diligently to advocate for the canal's maintenance and restoration. *Courtesy of the Friends of the Delaware Canal.*

hopes of providing continuing and united support. The caucus included State Senator Joe Conti; Dave Heckler as chairperson; six assemblymen; three state senators; Jim Greenwood, who was then a United States congressman; and then–lieutenant governor Mark Schweiker, who would become the forty-fourth governor of Pennsylvania in 2001. The mission of the caucus was to identify governmental agencies and other organizations that could help the canal, provide advocacy and assist in planning and coordinating activities that would impact the canal—always with the objective that it would be structurally sound and fully watered and used for programs that would educate and provide recreational activities and environmental protection.

The organization has received numerous awards for its work, including four Take Pride in Pennsylvania Awards and three consecutive Take Pride in America Awards. It also received a grant for signage along the canal and raised $100,000 for a long-arm track excavator during a "Pledge for the Dredge" project to begin the much-needed dredging required to restore the channel.

This page: A case in the lock tender's house in New Hope displays artifacts that were found along the banks of the canal during restoration. *Courtesy of the Friends of the Delaware Canal.*

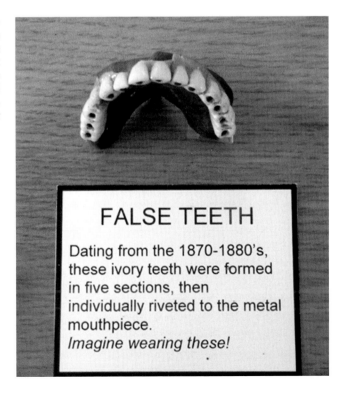

FALSE TEETH

Dating from the 1870-1880's, these ivory teeth were formed in five sections, then individually riveted to the metal mouthpiece.
Imagine wearing these!

The model of a lock at the FODC headquarters at Lock 11 demonstrates how a lock works. *Courtesy of the Friends of the Delaware Canal.*

When explaining why the FODC is so successful, Susan Taylor said:

> *When the canal was in commercial use, a community was created around it. The boatmen interacted with the locktenders, who in turn interacted with the local residents. There were stores and businesses that catered to the boatmen. Together they made the canal work. When the Friends of the Delaware Canal was founded, a "community" was again established to assist in the preservation of the canal, with everyone working together and caring about its welfare.*

The FODC continues its work diligently—just as the environment and weather continue to work against it. Flooding still plagues the canal, water leaks from it and the banks continue to collapse. Yet, it survives, and the FODC continues to advocate for it. "We still envision the entire sixty miles restored, but in the short term, we hope that sections of the canal will be repaired enough for people to enjoy it as it should be enjoyed," said Taylor.

The people who live along its towpath and berm, and the Pennsylvanians and tourists who visit the National Historic Landmark (and National

Hinge boats were the most common mode of transportation for anthracite coal and other cargo on the Delaware Division Canal. A model of a hinge boat is on display in the museum at Lock 11. *Courtesy of the Friends of the Delaware Canal.*

Murals portraying scenes of the canal age adorn the outer walls of a sitting area at Lock 11 in New Hope. *Courtesy of the Friends of the Delaware Canal.*

Today, the Delaware Canal serves as a picturesque haven for local residents, tourists, athletes and wildlife. *Author's collection.*

Water in the now idle Delaware Division Canal mirrors the beauty of surrounding trees and foliage. It is a natural aviary for birds and fowl, a home to several species of wildlife and a place where people go to find a quiet peace from a hectic world. *Author's collection.*

Recreation Trail) each year, cherish the historic waterway. They walk its towpath and never tire of its grace. It offers the beauty of nature in all weather and throughout the seasons, and presents an opportunity to savor creation in its lush flora, wading herons and diving kingfishers. It comes alive when the spring peepers hum their sweet songs, and it safeguards the nests of geese and swans. Deer lower their heads to drink of its waters. And children still run giggling, barefoot, on its velvety towpath.

In 1931, when the LC&N turned most of the Delaware Division Canal over to the people of Pennsylvania, poet Catherine Curran Smith published a verse in celebration in the *Intelligencer*. In part it read:

> *Its scenes of rural splendor*
> *Are portrayed by artists' touch;*
> *Its winter landscapes immortalized*
> *By the mighty Redfield's brush.*

> *It served mankind a century*
> *But now its days are spent*
> *We must preserve its beauty*
> *And leave nothing to repent.*

> *Oh, old canal, flow serenely on,*
> *And may beauty grace your way,*
> *Throughout the coming centuries,*
> *As she does at the present day!*[73]

From channel of industry to Pennsylvania treasure, the Delaware Division Canal, once congested with hinge boats, mules and scrappy canallers, now bestows a quiet peace and life-affirming splendor upon all who are drawn to it.

Notes

Chapter 1. Magic Canals: Past and Future

1. Needham and Ronan, *Shorter Science and Civilisation*, 5.
2. Find Articles, "The first contour transport canal—history of Chinese science," *UNESCO Courier*, http://findarticles.com/p/articles/mi_m1310/is_1988_Oct/ai_6955900.
3. Wikipedia, The Free Encyclopedia, s.v. "Emperor Yang of Sui," http://en.wikipedia.org/wiki/Emperor_Yang_of _Sui_China (accessed January 24, 2008).
4. Dale R. Lightfoot, "Syrian Qanat Romani," http://www.waterhistory.org/histories/syria (accessed January 25, 2008).
5. Wikipedia, The Free Encyclopedia, s.v. "Foss Dyke," http://en.wikipedia.org/wiki/Foss_Dyke (accessed January 24, 2008).
6. France in the United Kingdom, "Economics: Seine-Nord Europe canal: a new partnership with Europe," www.ambafrance-uk.org/Economics-Seine-Nord-Europe-canal.html (accessed January 30, 2008).
7. "About Canals," *999Canals*, http://www.999canals.com (accessed January 29, 2008).
8. Shank, *Amazing Pennsylvania Canals*, 10.

Chapter 2. From the Bowels of the Earth

9. Knies, *Coal on the Lehigh*, 4.
10. Ibid.
11. Karson, *Black Rock*, 2–3.
12. *Wikipedia, The Free Encyclopedia*, s.v. "Anthracite," http://en.wikipedia.org/wiki/Anthracite (accessed February 22, 2008).
13. Knies, *Coal on the Lehigh*, 7.

14. Hansell, *Josiah White*, 22.
15. Ibid., 29.
16. Ibid., 35.
17. Knies, *Coal on the Lehigh*, 37.
18. Hansell, *Josiah White*, 49.
19. Yoder, *Delaware Canal Journal*, 128.
20. Hansell, *Josiah White*, 79.
21. Ibid.
22. Richardson, *Memoir of Josiah White*, 108.
23. Hansell, *Josiah White*, 142.
24. Ibid., 146.
25. Stories from Pennsylvania History, "King Coal: Mining Bituminous," PennsylvaniaHistory.com, http://www.explorepahistory.com/story.php?storyId=30 (accessed February 7, 2008).
26. History Matters, "No Rest for the Weary: Children in the Coal Mines," http://historymatters.gmu.edu/d/5571 (accessed February 7, 2008).
27. Bartoletti, *Growing Up in Coal Country*, 27.
28. *Wikipedia, The Free Encyclopedia*, s.v. "Molly Maguires," http://en.wikipedia.org/wiki/Molly_Maguires (accessed February 5, 2008).
29. "Molly Maguires," *Everything2*, http://everything2.com/index.pl?node_id=1215887.
30. Karson, *Black Rock*, 57.

Chapter 3. Josiah White's Waterways

31. Lebegern, *Episodes in Bucks County*, 83.
32. Knies, *Coal on the Lehigh*, 66.
33. Hansell, *Josiah White*, 88.
34. Ibid., 89.
35. Zimmerman, *Pennsylvania's Delaware Division Canal*, 18.

Chapter 4. Locks and Their Keepers

36. *Collection of Papers*, 347.
37. Shank, *Amazing Pennsylvania Canals*, 113.
38. Baker, *Old Bucks County*, 16.
39. Gene Szostak, "Delaware Canal Brought a Growing Business to Bristol," *Bristol Pilot*, September 17, 1998.

Chapter 5. Beside the Busy Canal

40. Baker, *Old Bucks County*, 15.
41. *Wikipedia, The Free Encyclopedia*, s.v. "Devil's Half Acre," http:/ en.wikipedia.org/wiki/the_devil's_half_acre,_Pennsylvania (accessed March 21, 2008).
42. Green, *History of Bristol Borough*, 347.
43. Rivinus, *Lumberville*, 3.
44. Lee, *Tales the Boatmen Told*, 25.

Chapter 6. Snappers and Stiff Boats

45. Early River and Harbor Works, "Navigation Above Tide Water," United States Army Corps of Engineers, www.usace.army.mil/publications/ misc/un16/c-11.pdf, 74.
46. Ibid., 1,201.
47. Davis, *History of Bucks County*, 1,202.
48. R. Francis Rapp, "Lehigh and Delaware Division Canal Notes," *Collection of Papers*, 601.
49. Ibid., 600.
50. Ibid., 603.

Chapter 7. The Mules

51. Henry and Dennis, *Album of Horses*, 99.
52. Ibid., 101.
53. Bartoletti, *Growing Up in Coal Country*, 41.
54. Ibid., 44.
55. Yoder, *Delaware Canal Journal*, 179.
56. Ibid., 181.

Chapter 8. The Canallers

57. Project for Active Teaching of American History in Region 4, Summer Seminar, "Facts About Immigration," www.path.coe.uh.edu/ seminar2002/week2/immigrant_facts.html (accessed January 17, 2008).
58. Bartholomew and Metz, *Delaware and Lehigh Canals*, 125.

59. John T. Humphrey, "Life in Mid-Eighteenth Century Pennsylvania," About.com: Genealogy, http://genealogy.about.com/library/authors/uchumphreyb.htm (accessed February 23, 2008).

60. Davis, *History of Bucks County*, 898.

61. Rapp, "Canal Notes," *Collection of Papers*, 604.

62. Landreth, *War Times*, 6.

63. Henry R. Darling, "Canal People and Towpath Mules Hauled Coal 108 Miles to Big City," *The Bulletin*, n.d.

64. Pearl R. Nye, "The Old Skipper," The Library of Congress, American Memory, http://memory.loc.gov/ammem/collections/nye/index.html (accessed March 2, 2008).

65. Yoder, *Delaware Canal Journal*, 144.

66. Ibid., 192.

67. Ibid., 170.

Chapter 9. Human Cargo

68. Zimmerman, *Pennsylvania's Delaware Division Canal*, 38.

Chapter 11. Beautiful Impressions

69. "Fern I. Coppedge The Philadelphia Ten," James A. Michener Art Museum, http://www.michenermuseum.org/bucksartists/artist.php?artist=62&page=214 (accessed March 14, 2008).

Chapter 12. National Historic Landmark

70. Wartenberg and Luiso, *Delaware Canal*, 24.

71. Zimmerman, *Pennsylvania's Delaware Division Canal*, 126.

72. Ibid., 127.

73. Ibid.

Bibliography and Resources

Baker, Troy. *Old Bucks County: The Historic Delaware Valley.* Vol. I, Issue III. 1992.

Bartholomew, Ann, and Lance Metz, comp. and res. *Delaware and Lehigh Canals: A Pictorial History of the Delaware and Lehigh Canals.* Second edition. Easton, PA: Canal History and Technology Press, 2005.

Bartoletti, Susan Campbell. *Growing Up in Coal Country.* Boston: Houghton Mifflin Company, 1996.

Battle, J.H., ed. *History of Bucks County Pennsylvania.* Chicago: A. Warner and Co., 1887.

Coan, Peter Morton. *Ellis Island Interviews: In Their Own Words.* New York: Checkmark Books, 1997.

A Collection of Papers Read Before the Bucks County Historical Society. Vol. IV. Riegelsville, PA: Frackenthal Publication Fund, 1917.

Crumin, Timothy. "Fuel for the Fires: Charcoal Making in the Nineteenth Century." Connor Prairie Home. www.connerprairie.org/historyonline/fuel.html.

Davis, W.W.H. *The History of Bucks County Pennsylvania: From the Discovery of the Delaware to the Present Time.* Doylestown, PA: Democrat Book and Job Office Print, 1876.

Duess, Marie Murphy. *Colonial Inns and Taverns of Bucks County: How Pubs, Taprooms and Hostelries Made Revolutionary History.* Charleston, SC: The History Press, 2007.

Fall, Thomas. *Canalboat to Freedom.* Cuddebackville, NY: Neversink Valley Area Museum, 1966. Reprint, Foundation, Inc., 2008.

Green, Doran. *History of Bristol Borough in the County of Bucks, State of Pennsylvania.* Camden, NJ: C.S. Magrath, 1911.

Hansell, Norris. *Josiah White: Quaker Entrepreneur.* Easton, PA: Canal History and Technology Press, 1992.

Henry, Marguerite, and Wesley Dennis. *Album of Horses.* New York: Aladdin Books, 1993.

Karson, George Gershon. *Black Rock: Mining Folklore of the Pennsylvania Dutch.* New York: Arno Press, 1979.

Knies, Michael. *Coal on the Lehigh: 1790 to 1827*, Easton, PA: Canal History and Technology Press, 2001.

Landreth, Burnet. *War Times in Bristol: 1861–1865.* Bloomsdale House, n.d.

Lebegern, George F., Jr. *Episodes in Bucks County History: A Bicentennial Tribute 1776–1976.* Bucks County Historical Tourist Commission, n.d.

Lee, James. *Tales the Boatmen Told.* Exton, PA: Canal Press Incorporated, 1977.

McClellan, Robert J. *The Delaware Canal: A Picture Story.* New Brunswick, NJ: Rutgers University Press, 1967.

Needham, Joseph, and Colin A. Ronan. *The Shorter Science and Civilisation of China.* England: Cambridge University Press, 1978.

Parton, W. Julian. *The Death of a Great Company: Reflections on the Decline and Fall of the Lehigh Coal & Navigation Company.* Easton, PA: Canal History and Technology Press, 1986.

Richardson, Richard. *Memoir of Josiah White.* Philadelphia: J.B. Lippincott and Co., 1873.

Rivinus, Willis M. *Lumberville: 300 Year Heritage.* Privately printed, 2006.

Shank, William H., PE. *The Amazing Pennsylvania Canals.* 150th edition. York, PA: American Canal and Transportation Center, 1981.

Wartenberg, Steve, and Gian Luiso. *The Delaware Canal: Its Life, Its Legacy.* New Hope, PA: Friends of the Delaware Canal, 2000.

Yoder, C.P. *Delaware Canal Journal: A Definitive History of the Canal and the River Valley Through Which it Flows.* Bethlehem, PA: Canal Press Incorporated, 1972.

Zimmerman, Albright G. *Pennsylvania's Delaware Division Canal: Sixty Miles of Euphoria and Frustration.* Easton, PA: Canal History and Technology Press, 2002.

Resources

Friends of the Delaware Canal. New Hope, PA. www.fodc.org.

Gratz Gallery and Conservation Studio. New Hope, PA. www.gratzgallery.com.

Historic Langhorne Association. Langhorne, PA. www.hla.buckscom.net.

Margaret R. Grundy Memorial Library. Bristol, PA. www.buckslib.org/Bristol.

National Canal Museum. Easton, PA. www.canals.org.

New Hope Historical Society. New Hope, PA. www.newhopehistoricalsociety.org.

Pennsylvania Department of Environmental Protection, Bureau of Mining and Reclamation. www.dep.state.pa.us/dep/deputate/minres/bmr/bmrhome.htm

Index

A

Act for the Gradual Abolition of Slavery 117
anthracite coal 26, 27, 30, 44, 75, 78

B

Black Bass Hotel 71
Board of Canal Commissioners 45, 47, 50, 53
breaker boys 37

C

canalboats 80
Centre Bridge Inn 69
Coinage Act of 1873 137
Continental Tavern 16, 122
Coryell, Lewis S. 51

D

Delaware and Lehigh Navigation Canal National Heritage Corridor 142
Devil's Half-Acre 66
Durham, Robert 78
Durham boat 78
Durham Furnace 59, 78, 102

E

Erie Canal 21, 45, 47, 108

F

flood/freshet 52, 70, 71, 127, 128, 129, 139, 141
Foss Dyke 19

Franklin, Benjamin 20, 27, 117
Friends of the Delaware Canal 11, 16, 142, 143, 146

G

Ginder, Philip 25, 26, 27
Golden Pheasant Inn 71
Grand Canal 19
Greenwood, James C. 142, 144

H

Hauto, George F.A. 29, 31, 44
Hazard, Erskine 29, 30, 31, 32, 36, 44, 45, 137

I

Indiana Yearly Meeting 36
Industrial Revolution 20, 22, 26, 27, 37, 42, 75, 101, 107, 137
Ivory soap 73, 74

K

King George II 48

L

Lehigh Canal 47, 51, 81
Lehigh Coal and Navigation Company (LC&N) 32, 34, 36, 43, 44, 49, 50, 52, 67,
    71, 73, 81, 92, 109, 115, 137, 138–141
Lehigh Coal Mine Company (LCMC) 27, 28, 31
Lehigh Navigation Company 29, 31
Lehigh River 28, 32, 34, 35, 140
lock tenders 14, 54, 58–63, 98, 102, 104, 105, 107, 109, 114, 146

M

Magic Canal of China 17, 19
Mauch Chunk 25, 31, 34, 42, 43, 53, 65, 73, 78–82, 90, 91, 107, 115, 123
McParlan, James 42
Mitchell, Millard C. 120, 123
Molly Maguires 42
mules 32, 85–87, 89, 90, 92, 96
mule drivers 39, 69, 86, 103, 105, 135

N

National Canal Museum 15, 96
New Hope artists 131, 132, 133, 135
New Hope Canal Boat Company 16, 70, 135

nippers 38
Nye, Captain Pearl R. 108

P

Penn, William 11, 20, 22, 25, 75, 76, 98, 99, 117
Pennsylvania Assembly 45, 117

Q

Quaker 22, 29, 34, 35, 36, 117, 123

R

Roman canals 19
Roosevelt State Park 140

S

Seine-Nord Europe Canal 20
Smith, Catherine Curran 149
spraggers 38
Switchback Railroad 32
Swynford, Katherine 19

T

Tottorato, Rosemary 92

U

underground railroad 118, 120
Union Paper Mills 51

W

Washington, George 20, 21, 24, 69, 78, 86
Washington's Crossing 11, 73
Weiss, Jacob 25, 26, 27
White, Josiah 29–32, 34–36, 44, 45, 47, 49, 50, 91, 115, 128, 137

Visit us at
www.historypress.net